Tom Owen-Towle could have a spirited debate with Dylan Thomas. The Welsh romantic poet who urged us "Do not go gentle into that good night..." but instead to "Rage, rage against the dying of the light" would encounter a gentle soul in Reverend Tom who offers here instead a path to peaceful transition. Our author's trail meanders into Haiku, Tanka, and Zen poetry, the Asian art forms of spare words and robust meaning. In this meditative volume, Owen-Towle takes us by the hand to comfort and cajole, shepherd and steer, accompany and attend, for we are all in this certain aging together.

His wish for the closing of our spiritual and spirited journey is an invitation to a meaningful pilgrimage, one that embraces the uphill climb that leaves us breathless as well as the skid down the other side that elicits a hearty cheer, one that takes in the views of each curve before pausing at the pinnacle.

Burning and raving at the closing of our days versus purposefully contemplating a mindful dying would seem at first like two opposing perspectives. Yet, I imagine both authors agreeing over a cup of tea (or a toddy) that life is for living, for moving among the sacred forest with wild abandon as well as reverence, for seeing with blinding sight as well as with joyful surrender. The poets' rhythms may be vastly different, but both refrains challenge us to don a full consciousness.

Thomas' poem belts out a stormy chorus. Reverend Tom's book, this book, serenades with a serene lullaby.

—Dr. January Riddle is a Communications Professor and Founder of Write Doubt Communications Coaching. She is also co-author of *The Bridge Called Respect: Women and Men Joining as Allies*

Because death entered the world as the partner of sex, we humans are destined to die, a reality that's so disturbing we spend our lives denying it. Shall we go out kicking and screaming, or gracefully and gratefully? If we are blessed to make it to old age, we have time to become conscious and creative about our own uniquely unfolding path to the end.

With tried and true guide Tom Owen-Towle holding up a light and inviting us to follow, we can courageously face aging and dare to tread into death's unknown territory as if into a last great adventure. And whenever we're tempted to retreat, this book can become an extended meditation as we grow into the gifts of aging and dying.

There are precious jewels here. Be not afraid.

—Rev. Gail Collins-Ranadive is the author of eight books of nonfiction, including best book finalist *Chewing Sand, An Eco-Spiritual Taste of the Mojave Desert* and *A Fistful of Stars, Communing with the Cosmos*, forthcoming in late 2018.

Growing All the Way to Our Grave

Conscious Aging
&
Mindful Dying

Tom Owen-Towle

Flaming Chalice
P R E S S

Flaming Chalice Press™
3303 Second Ave.
San Diego, CA 92103
Tel: (619) 933-1121
Website: www.tomo-t.com

10 9 8 7 6 5 4 3 2 1
First English Edition 2018

ISBN 13: 978-0-692-05647-9

Library of Congress Catalog Card Number: 2018900472

Cover and book design by CenterPointe Media
www.CenterPointeMedia.com

Dedication

to my noble and valiant peers

plus the youngers of the world who are also graying

and will someday croak…

may we all grow up, on, and out

with as much dignity as possible

Table of Contents

Prologue

Heaps of fine books on the physical and medical, legal and financial issues of aging already exist, so *Growing All the Way to Our Grave (Conscious Aging and Mindful Dying)* pivots upon the spiritual assignment of seniors completing our lives as purposefully as possible. Clearly, most golden agers yearn to stay evergreen and harvesting to the end. Before we *rest* in peace, we strive to *live* in peace…daily. Hopefully, this book of poetic reflections will assist you in balancing self-possession and solitude, questing and soul-work, joy and service, anguish and hope, bequest and surrender.

Growing All the Way to Our Grave finishes with lyrical hunches about dying, tendered from the purview of one still bouncing. There's mindful meditation, mindful eating, mindful parenting, mindful walking, mindful suffering, and, yes, there's mindful dying. It transpires whenever we ponder, plan, and prepare for our own mortality, both philosophically and good-humoredly. The observation of author Annie Dillard is hauntingly apt:

> Write as if you were dying. At the same time, assume you write for an audience consisting solely of terminal patients. That is, after all the case. What if you begin writing as if you knew you would die soon? And what could you say to a dying person that would not enrage by its triviality?

Writing launched my life as well, being absolutely integral to my formation as a young boy. My ever-watchful mother intuited that her squirt of a son hankered for some sort of tiny pad and pencil on the bed stand, so that he might scrawl stuff at the end of the day or perhaps craft notes for the forthcoming morn. I used various pads and pencils throughout my school days. I wish I still had my countless scribbles to perceive how my life evolved. What might one label this nascent practice: a habit, an obsession, or a "positive addiction," to employ psychologist William Glasser's favorable phrase? Whatever the term, this craving arrived early; it's my main mode of traipsing through the world, of "con-*solid*-ating" my scattered emotions and notions, of corralling life's zaniness. I resonate with author Brian Doyle's perspective:

> Some of us build houses, companies, reputations, tribes of children; some of us make small essays in small rooms. Thrashing toward light with a sharp pen is what writers do.

In 2016, I turned 75, which is the explicit age when, according to Hindu culture, we enter the *vanaprastha* or "forest-dweller" life-stage. We hand over major household tasks to the "youngers," stem desires of acquisition and attainment, and assume a greater mentoring role. It signals a potential epoch of self-realization, of summation, of tackling nagging spiritual concerns, of shedding, of legacy...all of which is what *Growing All the Way to Our Grave* chases. Of course, I might have waited until I turned 80 or 85 or even later to convey my last hurrah or hallelujah, but you just don't know how many annual go-arounds you get, do you? Both my dad and father-in-law died at 81 ½, the average life-expectancy for men. Who can guarantee that I will live longer than they did?

My two best male friends died during the past year, one eagerly wanting to halt a pain-saturated existence, and the other one, passing away prematurely of an unexpected illness. This present volume was born out of my own grief and "thrashing toward light." We had covenanted for both of these brothers to speak at my memorial service, but, lamentably, I ended up speaking at theirs. This duo of heart-wrenching deaths has placed my own mortality front and center. Accordingly, this book furnishes a modest tribute to Nathan's and Paul's ongoing presence in my remaining years on earth. It aspires to validate the sentiment of Thornton Wilder:

> *There is a land of the living and a land of the dead.*
> *The bridge is love; the only truth, the only survival.*

Yes, only love conquers death. These buddies won't return in person, only in love. Only in love do I have them still.

This last two-year stretch of time has also been one of momentous pilgrimages for my wife Carolyn and me: noteworthy excursions into the heartland of China, Japan, and Mexico. Fortuitously, these three foreign nations found me excavating a passion that started when I turned 50, while residing in Germany: the composition of free verse. During the ebb and flow of these recent, sacred life-treks, I migrated from journal observations into scripting rough-hewn poems. I've grown fascinated with Haiku, Tanka, and Zen poetry, zones of imagination which found their origins in Asia.

In fact, during my trip to China, I learned that poetry was one of the established forms of creativity all educated Chinese were expected to master. One's proficiency as a poet was even tested in civil service exams, and erstwhile Chinese emperors prided themselves on their ability to pen refined verse.

A fresh jewel emerged as well: "the death poem," a genre of poetry that developed in the literary traditions of East Asian cultures, most prominently in Japan (called a *jisei* or farewell poem). This solemn practice reflects deep-rooted origins in Zen Buddhism. These verses classically couple the imminent death of the author along with evocative, scathingly honest, observations upon life.

Here's a *jisei* by Kozan Ichikyo, Zen monk, composed in 1360:

> *Empty-handed I entered the world*
> *Barefoot I leave it.*
> *My coming, my going—*
> *Two simple happenings*
> *That got entangled.*

Not wishing to wait until my own death knell, I've chosen to muse upon my transience and forthcoming finale, right here and now. Indeed, writing death poems, surely from a distance, is an art accessible to all seniors. The other day, at the beginning of a worship service, when a fellow attendee asked me what I was currently up to, I replied: "Well, among other stuff, I'm composing Haiku poems, often on the theme of mortality." At the end of the service, but an hour later, Theresa had proudly carved one of her own:

> *death comes for everyone*
> *why should it be a surprise*
> *when it comes for you?*

One more confession. After I die, I want to be remembered, at least for a spell and by some folks. I seem to suffer from a hyperactive survival drive. Some of us get a modicum of life-extension through generous material gifts. Other people receive recognition through the memories or actions of offspring. And we writers garner a smidgen of immortality through words. At least that's the hope.

⇚⎈

> *A poem is a temple—or a green field—a place to enter,*
> *and in which to feel.*
> *A poem was made not just to exist, but to speak, to be*
> *company.*
> —Mary Oliver

My previous books have essentially been comprised of concise essays; but why not, as my own life-span shortens, turn to a pithier mode of composition? Therefore, I've decided to communicate my wizened, mottled wisdom through the vehicle of poetry. Hence, the third and fourth segments of *Growing All the Way to Our Grave* will major in phrases and lines rather than in sentences, in *what is* more than amplified *whys* and *wherefores*. I've tried to delete most punctuation and capital letters while turning to an intuitive format.

My homestretch ruminations are compact and bare, reminiscent of Japanese poetic forms. The Japanese Haiku, frequently associated with and used by Zen Buddhist monks and meditators, emphasizes the common and the unpretentious. Haiku is clothed in the plainest and most modest garment of but 17 (5-7-5) syllables and uses everyday elements for its subject matter. Being condensed, Haiku allows, nay forces, us to salute the fleeting impression, the undersized moment.

The Haiku tradition is comparatively recent, having been derived from Tanka in the late 1600's. Of all the songs and poems written throughout the 2000 year history of Japan, Tanka is the earliest classical form. Tanka poems contain 31 syllables, divided into five lines of 5-7-5-7-7 syllables.

A classic example of Tanka:
> *"What is truth?" I asked.*
> *One answered, "it's so and so."*
> *One said, "it is thus."*
> *But truth is not what they say;*
> *truth is really what they do.*

And a Tanka poem of my own, entitled "Freeing":

> *my crafting of poems*
> *not weird preoccupation*
> *neither fixation*
> *nor mere fascination*
> *rather...freeing of spirit*

One distinction needs to be clarified: while Haiku poetry focuses upon natural images, its relative, *sensryu*, salutes human dynamics. In this book, I invariably gravitate to the *sensryu* accent. I major more in values than in images. It's just the way I prefer to communicate. I'm an unrepentant meaning-maker.

However, the vast majority of the 300+ poems in *Growing All the Way to Our Grave* will derive from the Zen heritage which, although somewhat looser and more expansive in form than either Haiku or Tanka, still stresses austerity as well as the artistic engagement between our inner and outer worlds. Zen literally means "meditative absorption." In Taoism and Zen Buddhism, there is a ubiquitous lightness of spirit, a consciousness rarely encountered in our Western world. You may recall the critique, "stinking of Zen," a perennial reminder not to take ourselves either piously or earnestly (both of which I'm prone to do). Indeed, Zen practitioners focus modestly upon gradual maturation while eschewing sudden enlightenment.

Hence, I invite you to read this volume in a state of calm, reflectively yet with carefreeness, treating space breaks as enjoyable pauses. Perhaps one poetic reflection per day, read out loud, even several times, would prove to be a useful discipline. Sometimes parse every word, sometimes just soak.

Here is one of my own Zen odes to get us launched, called "*Growing the Soul*," germane to the thrust of this particular book:

> my body   *aches and crumbles*
>   *my mind*   *filters and flitters*
> *my friends*   *are dying*
> *my world*   *is shrinking*
>   *inexorably*
> *still*   *my soul*   *hankers*
>   *to grow*
>   *and*   *it will*   *as it can*
>   *with*   *ample*   *assistance*
>   *from*   *beyond*

Oh, by the way, you'll be able to detect, by length, which poems are Haiku, Tanka, or Zen; furthermore, all are titled, and most arrive with an opening quotation. My verses are quite evenly distributed between aging and dying, although I consider living-and-dying to be hallowed mysteries—yoked and interwoven in human existence. Indeed, practicing thanatologists note that some folks are never more alive than when they are dying. Consequently, in my conscious aging section, I reference topics of sorrow, illness, even perishing. Likewise, in the final portion on mindful dying, I imagine potential forms of abundant and abiding life.

This array of poems aspires to be varied, both in gist and timbre: personal yet philosophical, poignant yet playful. May my free-flowing verses stretch your psyche, tickle your fancy, trouble your spirit, thicken your destiny, and strengthen your resolve to live more intentionally and die more gracefully...or as my friend says: "May we keep hoeing to the end of the row!"

Growing Like a Tree

In Japan, my life-mate Carolyn and I strolled the cobblestone pathways where Japanese poets such as Dogen, Basho, and Ikkyu likely sauntered...pondering and composing in centuries past...amidst groves of trees such as this 800-year-old camphor growing on a moss-covered slope at the Shoren-in Buddhist temple in Kyoto.

i thank You God for most this amazing
day: for the leaping greenly spirits of trees
and a blue true dream of sky: and for everything
which is natural which is infinite which is yes.
—e. e. cummings

On the cover of *Growing All the Way to Our Grave* resides a symbol that parallels our human vocation to the growing of a tree. Throughout this collection of poems on conscious aging and mindful dying, I've explored the mystery and majesty of the tree, drawing upon our kinship with these natural marvels. The *Tree of Life* heralds a widespread and evocative archetype in world mythologies and religions. As maverick theologian and cosmologist Matthew Fox notes:

> *Sacred groves are a universal phenomenon. Almost everywhere in the world the beginnings of social and religious life took place under trees. Every Greek deity was linked to a particular tree species and worshipped under it, such as the laurel consecrated to Apollo, the myrtle tree to Aphrodite, the olive to Athena, and the pine tree to Pan. What we today label as gods were originally the spirits of trees to whom good will and gratitude were bestowed.*

You may recall that Mark, in the earliest Christian gospel, imagines: "I see people as trees, walking..." (8:24). Naturalist Fred Hageneder seconds the match: "Humans and trees share an upright, vertical orientation. We walk, they stand. We move and change; they remain the quiet center of *being*." And, of course, our life-spans differ; trees sometimes live for eons (the bristlecone pine can live 5,000 years, making it the oldest individually growing organism on the planet), whereas we humans are destined to 90 or so years, if duly blessed. Nevertheless, we're the sturdiest of allies, exuding a synergetic bond, whether in fairy tales or during our respective, earthly stints.

Note how we humans and trees sprout in similar fashion. As elders and crones, our homestretch drive is to stay in motion, to keep on keeping on, to grow in multiple directions: *inwardly* (engaging in deeper contemplation and self-appraisal); *outwardly* (connecting to and collaborating with fellow creatures, expanding our horizons, and sustaining our environs); *upwardly* (celebrating, elevating our spirits, surveying the beyond, breathing the heavens); and *downwardly* (probing our lineage, descending into the netherworld of unavoidable sorrow and torment, and returning to the soil from whence we came). Sometimes we seniors navigate these various routes, piecemeal; at other times, we traverse many zones simultaneously. Now and again, it's impossible to pinpoint the specific direction of a personal transition, such as when one dies. Is death essentially a downward or an upward spiral, or a mystical combination of the two?

There are additional comparisons between every tree and every human being.

A tree without *roots* or historical continuity topples easily. Our "rootage" as human beings is both broad and deep. Broad in that our tree receives nutrients from the sod of sundry environments and backgrounds. For instance, you and I garner sagacity from the East and West, from the North and South, from the humus of countless religious and secular sources. My most recent foray into the heartland of Mexico was, in large measure, to connect with the roots, branches, and leaves of my heritage, to unearth the bloodline connection with my grandmother Clorinda Ramirez, who came to live with us early in my childhood, following the shocking suicide of her husband. Deep in the drift that our nourishment comes through living out our symbols and stories in singular ways, roots bespeak an expansive, subterranean network of interweaving elements: natural, human, and divine. We earthlings are fed at our very roots.

Remember that roots change, too. As the tree of our peculiar destiny grows taller and wider, the roots grow deeper and broader. Although roots vary quite a lot in their systems, their nutritional function persists.

According to the Hebrew heritage, Adam emerged from the earth. His origin was moist, dirty, even slimy. Like Adam, we were fashioned not out of light or fire, but sludge. We are children of mud, and we will eventually revert to our ancestral home: the soil, the ground, the grave.

The *trunk* represents our core (deriving from the French word *coeur*, meaning heart), our inner identity, our hub. All that transpires during our cumulative days and nights is processed through the trunk. When I ponder a tree trunk, I think of thickness and sturdiness. The trunk centers, holds, and supports the entire system.

The *bark* of the tree is the living, finite exterior of our corpus, the pelt of our being, so to speak. Taking good, reasonable care (what I call "temple maintenance") of our carcass is not a luxury but an essential task for healthy, holy creatures.

The *branches* of the tree reach out in kinship with and compassion toward our fellow travelers: be they animate or inanimate entities, plants or deities. Families are precisely like branches on a tree, hence the moniker, *family tree*. We morph and mature in distinct ways, yet our roots remain as one. Our branches grow upward as well as outward. Branches extend to sources of wisdom, power, and fuel beyond our control, even our comprehension. Branches reach skyward in gratitude, awe, ecstasy, humility, and longing. Indeed, trees are innately lured to every ray of sun or drop of rain. Trees often sway and twist, bend and bow, before they break. Trees rise and soar, exhibit loftiness, and suggest transcendence. Reflect a moment upon a tree ascending upward. As the yarn goes: a small shrub, growing next to a tall pine, looks down at the ground and observes: "Look how tall I am." The tall pine gazes at the sky and sighs: "Look how short I am!" It's all a matter of perspective.

The *leaves*, the flowers, the fruit of our trees herald the seasonal shifts in our chronicles. Growing individuals undergo the dramatic vicissitudes of winter and spring, summer and fall. We blossom, we're lush, we drop leaves, and we're barren. As James Fowler and Sam Keen reflect in their book *Life-Maps*: "Maybe the leaves are my aspirations, my hopes, my wishes, the best I can be, the closest I can come to the sun, to the universe, to the stars, to the wind."

Yea, both our solitary and communal lives are periodically uprooted, rotted, broken, even crucified. Other times we're strong, lavish, or exalted. Through it all, unless prematurely felled, our tree lives on, endures, until it reenters the ground from which it arose, or prolongs as a stump nursing additional growth. Moreover, all along the way, our trees must be regularly pruned and shaped by devout gardeners. Our very sustenance banks on the benevolence of external forces, both human and ecological.

Growing All the Way to Our Grave summons us to evolve all our days and nights on earth: growing inwardly, outwardly, upwardly, and downwardly. Each direction constitutes a sacred movement. During the cyclical span of existence on earth, our objective remains stretching homeward, onward, forward. Our family friend, James Hubbell, a consummate artist and poet, has branded his foundation *Ilan-Lael*, which translates: "We are trees growing, belonging to God, with our branches in the sky and our roots in the earth, symbols of spirit and matter united in form." And, frankly, what sort of growth might transpire once we've entered our tombs or been scattered afield? No one knows what lies beyond the grave.

My life-mate Carolyn and I have fashioned a personalized symbol of significance for our marriage, family, and ministerial partnership. We call it: *Growing Like a Tree*. This religious symbol adorns our pastoral robes created by Carolyn's mother, Mary Baskerville Sheets, and the same talisman was cast in gold by Carolyn's sibling, Tony, and has graced our necks ever since our marital vows 44+ years ago.

This precious pendant aims to keep our life humble (grounded in humor, the humus, and humaneness) and in energizing touch with the fierce and abiding yin-yang opposites (male-female, internal-external, good-evil, up-down, joy-sorrow, light-dark, and more) within ourselves and the universe. It spurs us to grow tall and proud, venture out on limbs, appreciate our blessed views, and resemble the spirit of the numinous poet, Wendell Berry: "Be like a tree in pursuit of your cause: stand firm, grip hard, thrust upward, bend to the winds of heaven and learn tranquility."

In one fashion or another–sometimes overtly, other times, obliquely–this principal metaphor of "growing like a tree" informs my spray of poems examining conscious aging and mindful dying. I've composed, then released, these verses, essentially as the spirit moved me; so, may you enjoy them as the spirit moves you. They portend the valiant human effort to keep growing up and growing onward…all the way to our own grave.

Joyce Kilmer crafted the well-known poem: *I think that I shall never see a poem lovely as a tree.* His point is unquestionably true. A tree is God's creation. A poem is a human construction. This book aspires to bridge the two.

Conscious Aging

Age puzzles me. I thought it was a quiet time.
My 70's were interesting and fairly serene,
but my 80's are passionate.
I grow more intense as I age.
—FLORIDA SCOTT-MAXWELL

AWAKEN!

If you're not dead yet, you're not done yet.

—Elizabeth Gilbert

awaken   o my   slumbering   spirit
being   laid-back   aimless
enticed   to indolence   and   indulgence
does   not befit   a   wisdom keeper
safeguarding   tribal   savvy   and   survival

prime   for   your   latest   lasting   chore

creation aches for twin fuels
passion and compassion

plants   animals   neighbors
all   relatives

seek

energetic   gentle   transforming   touch
thy   touch

DESERT JOY

The wilderness and the dry land shall be glad;
the desert shall rejoice and blossom like a rose.
—Isaiah 35:1

all is barren   bone-dry wasteland

nothing seems to bud   where you've burrowed

keep mulching soil
cultivating soul

marvels occur

who knows when

fruits   and   foliage
may   flower

even
in   your   desert?

OCCASION FOR REVERENCE

*I should be content to look at a mountain for what it is
and not as a comment on my life.*
—David Ignatow

an incorrigible meaning-maker

doubly cursed   by temperament and trade

spinning majestic redwoods into homiletical yarn

converting   vistas into   platitudes

such as   "standing beneath this marvel of

towering rock   my furies are quieted…"

mountains   range   on

occasion   for   reverence

FOREST-DWELLER

I quietly gaze into the depths of a forest
and see nothing save beauty and peace...
Seeing from inside the seeing,
I drink the dark riches of the woods.
—CASS ADAMS

forest-dweller now

plotting hours more prudently

in or out of woods

mostly gazing and grazing

beneficial daily fare

EARTHBOUND

no stargazer

Confucius was too absorbed in the wonders of Earth

to expound on heaven or angels or eternity

following   in   footsteps   of   Chinese   mentor

we   revel   in natural splendor
brave   its   quakes
focus   upon planet preservation
ripen   into   an honorable species

savor   and   serve

exquisite   earthly   cycle

DRY GARDEN LANDSCAPE

at   the Ryonaki Zen Temple   in   Kyoto, Japan   (built in 1450)
        there   stands an exquisite   dry garden   consisting

        of 15 rocks   expertly laid out   in a softly raked bed
                    of white gravel
    a symbolic expression   of   our spacious universe
                    within a restricted space

            i assume   a meditative seat

                    two lessons arise

        first
                no one   can view   all 15 rocks   at once
        hence   our human perspective   is forever limited

                    second

            stones stay   we go

MOM AND DAD

What a child doesn't receive, they can seldom later give.
—P. D. James

although   parents   are   long   gone
1987 and 2004

on   the   84th anniversary   of   their   wedding

i   shower   them   with   gratitude

for eyes   that truly   saw   me

for hands   safe and comforting

for hearts   staunch in principles   pliant in tastes

for activating   my soul and voice

for   demonstrating   fruitfulness

wherever   planted

Growing All the Way to Our Grave

NOW…ALWAYS

In old age, they still produce fruit; they are
always green and full of sap.
—Psalm 92:14

now is season of

peace-making … justice-building

mercy and kindness

virtues for every reason

always   purposeful   always

XIN

the Chinese word for mind and heart is actually one and the same
Xin

prompting   elders everywhere

to unbridle   a mindful heart

a heartful mind

optimal way   to voyage   homeward

ENSO

Japanese word   meaning   "circular form"
    supreme symbol of enlightenment in Zen Buddhism

as modern-day Buddhist priest and teacher John Stevens reminds

our individuality is expressed   in the *ensos*   we brush
        whether drawn   in the air   or   in the dirt
            one bold stroke   or two half circles
                thick   or   thin

    while   none of our crafted creations   are perfect
        this spiritual discipline   suggests
            sacred   calligraphy
            rounded   existence

    i deem to sketch   an enso   daily
        on my   petite   portable   Buddha board

MOST BEAUTIFUL EXPERIENCE

The most beautiful experience we can have is the mysterious.
It is the fundamental emotion which stands at the
cradle of true art and true science.
—ALBERT EINSTEIN

quintessential   20th century   German-Swiss   physicist
            steeped   in   science
                            yet
        the good doctor stirred to claim
                mystery
                    as   "most beautiful experience"

sense of wonder   hurling us   skyward
    sense of astonishment   birthing hallelujahs
        sense of awe   driving us to knees

            as colleague muses
        "in mystery we are born
                    in mystery we live
                            in mystery we die"

CONSTANT TRUTH

Empathy is the most revolutionary of emotions.
—Gloria Steinem

resentment   erodes

bitterness   diminishes

empathy   strengthens

SAME KEY

To everyone is given the key to the gates of heaven
and the same key opens gates of hell.
—CHINESE PROVERB

fog sets in

winds drone eerily

aging wayfarers   nervously finger

lone   key

alluring   gates   beckon

easy now

it's nightfall

every   verdict

tallies

5% RULE

beat or not   frazzled or not

no excuse   for   being   listless   bystander

psychiatrist's prompt   single most important factor for
conscious aging

flexibility   changeability   adaptability

henceforth   heed   the   5%   rule

loosen some soil

fertilize a tad

prune hanging twig

repot nearby plant

CALLING ALL ELDERS

God has need of a person here.
—Ralph Waldo Emerson

homespun lessons fall short
tribal   know-how   tired
                                        call in the elders
                seasoned cradlers of entire village
bringing to full stature
            yet   another   child

                        olders   bidding   youngers

to take walks   around lakes
            spring-clean   gardens   closets   psyches
                    think   soulfully
        manage   successive   approximations
            discern   when   to   make   self small
                and   when   to   be   large presence
seed   plantlets
                        be   both   stroker   and   ruffler

                elder   wisdom   essential

WU-WEI

As in nature, the tree that bends with the wind survives, and the water that yields to the rock in its path, eventually wears down the hard stone, so, too, the wise person knows that often to yield is to be preserved whole.

—Lao Tzu

flowing   bendable

effortless   spontaneous

eldering   pathway

ENOUGH CHAOS

There must be enough chaos
in one's life to give birth to dancing stars.
—FRIEDRICH NIETZSCHE

for this taut   tight-assed   traveler
tiny slices of confusion   disorder
stick out   unnerve
during senior stint

imperfect shaves

forgotten   duties
adult children   scrambling
flabby   girth
hiccups
relational squabbles
tremors
just enough chaos

clear-cut   indicators
that   life   isn't   pre-set   smooth   static

as   dance   descends

HUSBANDRY

during my homestretch

above all else

i wish to

be   a devoted   delightful   diligent   husband
            of everyone   and   everything

within my expansive household

then   as each challenge   requires   branching out

i wish to

be   a judicious steward   of   all   earthly resources

of   all   my   remaining

moments

CAROLYN

You are my harvest. You are my business.
You are my magnitude and bond.
—Gwendolyn Brooks

harvest
  although we birthed none of our own
    we've reared and been reared by four offspring   still
  our co-ministry has also produced a hefty yield

  since we yoked on October 26, 1970
    we've been one another's main *business*
     covenant of thickest consequence

magnitude
  matches as well
  for no one has proven more sizable and
  momentous
    in molding my course than you

bond
grows inwardly outwardly upwardly downwardly
   all the way
     to our respective graves

HOME

The most important work you and I will ever do will
be within the walls of our own home.
—Harold Lee

home-based   labor
recreation
sweat and tears

never cease

vacuuming our room
hosting meals
repairing shingles   and   fractures
schooling   reunionizing
playing table games
soothing sensitive spots
tilling   turfs   germinating   orchards

whatever   roads you cover   places you roam

never   ever   stop   going   home
being
home

IF ONLY...

If only I may grow firmer, simpler, quieter, warmer.
—DAG HAMMARSKJÖLD (1905-1961)

superlative   Swedish diplomat   economist   author
second Secretariat-General of the United Nations
killed in plane crash   en route   to cease-fire negotiations
stolen   away   too   early

whether   you   or   i   get   15 or   30 or   60 or   90 or
more years

Dag's   pledge   persists   insists

grow firmer

simpler

quieter

warmer

FORBIDDEN CITY

Be self-sufficient but not isolated.
When the king of China closed the borders,
centuries of stagnation and decadence began.
—DENG MING-DAO

walled compound
impenetrable heart of Chinese empire
off limits   to commoners   for more than 500 years
rules   loosened   today

as   we   amble   headlong

what remains   off-limits   forbidden
in   our   country
in   our   home
in   our   heart

clamoring
to be   unlocked   opened up   set free?

BEHOLDEN

We build on foundations we did not lay. We warm ourselves at fires we did not light. We sit in the shade of trees we did not plant. We drink from wells we did not dig. We profit from persons we did not know.
—Peter Raible

indebted

bound

beholden

obliged

only   one   suitable   rejoinder

live

thankfully

MAY KINDNESS SWELL

The chair, the air, the paper, and the street; you must be kind to them.
—DICK ALLEN

as   a   geezer   may   my   better   angels   prevail

may   my   horizons   objects   experiences   of   kindness   swell

may   my list   of   kith and kin

mushroom

encircling   strangers   nature   material

animals   foes   divinities

ZEN

Zen practice   is   chiefly

chopping wood and carrying water

chopping wood and carrying water

doing   the basics   of existence

repeatedly

in   sustainable fashion

performing simplest tasks

with   gumption   and   grace

sage guidance

for   youngers   middlers   elders

GRIT

Choose what you want, then pay for it.
—Robert Bly

to see   every day and night   through to the end

    to see a breakage mended

       to see a dream modified

          to see a shrub cropped

            to see a chasm gulfed

     demands

  most   unsung

       virtue   in   human   arsenal

FENG-SHUI

Chinese priority

aligning   self and surroundings   in pleasing arrangement

mysterious art of placement

starts with furniture

then alongside flora and fauna

then in conjunction with animals

then forging linkages with humans

of distinct hues

heritages

habits

hardships

feng-shui

finally   tackles   sternest   test

the   decisive orientation

harmonizing   our own   interior domain

MUDDY WATER

May we exist like a lotus, at home in the muddy water.
Thus we bow to life as it is.
—Zen

every land   falls short   of   noble promises
    every land   exudes   beauty and ugliness
      every land   touts   its   historical   achievements
        hides   its   manifest   disasters
every land promotes   its own version   of justice and freedom
      yet falls   far short   in reality

   one   eldering task   overrides

sleuth out   the curious gifts and   wonders   of   every land
   while   never ignoring   its travesties and terrors

    then   with   diplomatic devotion

     deliver   a respectable bow

    waist deep   in   muddy water

MARVELS

So every good tree bears good fruit…
—Matthew 7:17

ponder   the   bounteous benefits   of our relative   the tree

     at their finest
         they combat   climate change
muffle earsplitting sounds   block unsightly views
   conserve energy   save water
provide fruits   nuts   timber   medicine
     help prevent erosion
furnish critical habitat   for other species
as well as a space   for human retreat   and   playfulness
            moreover
patients heal faster   with fewer complications
when in view   of these elegant marvels

         comparisons are odious

     but   but   one has to wonder
if our human species is   carting   its weight   in
overall   ecological stream?
        are we doing   our full share   to make
   Earth   a *fairer*   (more beautiful and just)   habitat?

ME FOR ME

Illness is not a failure and pain is not a punishment.
Be <u>with</u> your pain, rather than <u>against</u> it…touching it deeply,
examining it, drawing the self-torture out of it by meeting
pain with tenderness and mercy—"me for me."
—Stephen and Ondrea Levine

ailing seniors   are encouraged   to befriend   our pain
as if   we were   gently soothing   a distressed child
holding it in   a calming   squeeze

breathing   lightly   into   the   direct seat   of   our ache

accompanying   each inhalation   and   exhalation with words
in   out   slow   deep   thanks yes   smile peace

summoning   the spirit of life and   love

to fill   our   body

with   healing   kindness

ERA OF DE-SIREMENT

When physical eyesight declines, spiritual eyesight increases.
—PLATO

call it what you will
re-tirement or re-wirement or re-firement as i prefer
you will know when you've entered
golden years

physical capacities wane
outreach shrinks
time is preoccupied

less with doing   what we should

more with doing   what we wish

realizing

at long last

an era of de-sirement

UNREASONABLE INTEREST

Our families are those people who maintain
an unreasonable interest in each other.
—ELLEN GOODMAN

intimacy crackles
    bloodlines incite
        like no other attachments

despite testy battles
    even ferocious splits

    vestiges   of   "unreasonable interest in each other"
        fasten
          linger

    discs along the same spine

SHUNYATA

Emptiness is not negative; it is letting go of
fixed ideas in order to go beyond them.
—Dainin Katagiri

Sanskrit term

meaning emptiness

not nothing   not nothingness
rather   full-bore openness   to   an   existence
freer from   external   unwanted   baggage

shunyata

imperative   to keep a corner of house
empty
for   sitting serenely   crooning intrepidly

reminder to keep a zone of mind
empty
for   relishing
life's   delicacies
and
mercies

ONLY CONNECT

Only connect…and the isolation that is life will die.
—E. M. FORSTER

only connect

with this pencil
that savannah
today's predicament
a pleasant prospect
a pedestrian
a gazebo
an agony

thyself

only connect

RAIN AND GRACE

To be fully human is to live with a concourse of emotions,
including life's joys and sorrows irremediably entwined.
Some hurts haunt a lifetime. Let's stop worrying
whether we've passed the grief test. Nobody does.
—Clarke Dewey Wells

gray panthers   are prompted   to weep some   every day
letting our tears   spill   wet   fertilize   the ground
staying moist   ample   juices flowing

in some Middle Eastern languages the words for *rain* and *grace*
are the same

without the dampness of anguish
life   delivers   tepid   arid   experiences

biblical admonition   rings true
"blessed are they who mourn, for they shall be comforted"

verily   verily   comfort visits   only those   gutsy   enough
to weep   openly   and   ongoingly

ENCHANTMENT

Where is your Self to be found?
Always in the deepest enchantment that you have experienced.
—Hugo von Hofmannsthal

afternoon of existence
is   period
when   our   maximum crop   can be reaped
fruitage   garnered   and   gathered in

when   custodians and conveyors   of sagacity
can   realize
enchantment

might   embrace
the   subtler charm and fizz
we missed in   earlier decades
of   chasing   clambering

this   very afternoon   you may be
favored
by   unforeseen   enchantment

GRAY PANTHER

Each night, when I go to sleep,
I die. And the next morning,
when I wake up, I am reborn.
—Mahatma Gandhi

aging   placidly

yet   no crotchety   zombie

elder   on   the   prowl

SITTING

Don't just do something, sit there.
—Sylvia Boorstein

sitting alone   still

breathing in   then   breathing out

eternity   now

WELL-DOING

Do not be weary in well-doing.
—GALATIANS 6:9

body grows weary
will

wear out

notwithstanding

time exists
challenges present

to let your life speak

be a well-doer

bake some bread
climb a tree
adopt a stray animal
craft a lyric
smile
laugh
cuddle
hum

DO THE DROPS

A soft answer turns away wrath,
but a harsh word stirs up anger.
—PROVERBS 15:1

occasionally　　　　　recoiling or squawking　　　　are in order

most of the time
especially　　　　during our　　　so-called　　　"brittle" years

obey　　　　　　　the meditation mantra

"Don't　Resist　Or　Push,　Soften"

do the drops

MY FIRST BUDDY

Merry meet, merry part, until we merry meet again.
—Wiccan greeting

Phil and Tom
　　brothers sparring affectionately
　　　　from cradle forward
　　　　　　healthy pugnacity
　　　no harm　　no foul

despite distinct personalities and quirks
shatterproof　　love　　sustains
both　are "light-workers"
　　both　exult　in sports
　　both　reveal　from　soulful zones
　　　　an utterly　irreplaceable　bond…
　　　　　　known longer　　than anyone　else　alive

reconnoitered　recently　for a couple days
in old　familiar　neighborhood haunts
meandering　　　　　　swapping prized memories
　　bearing/baring　challenge and comfort　for our denouements
　　　　　　kissing
　　　until we merry meet again

SI, SE PUEDE

*Rallying cry of Dolores Clara Fernandez Huerta, American
labor leader and civil rights activist (1930-) ... central to
the United Farm Workers in the 1960's and currently
to the immigrant rights movement.*

"Yes, we can...yes, it's doable"

dismantle patriarchy
become a truly inclusive and hospitable nation
confront white supremacy
effect environmental justice

yes, one can
yes, you can
yes, we can
yes, it can be done

day   by   day   by   day   by   day

until time runs out

RENEWAL

So we do not lose heart. Though our outer nature is wasting away,
our inner nature is being renewed every day.
—II CORINTHIANS 4:16

too much rest spells rust

emulate the tree
      explode skyward
           in search of   rays of sunlight   beads of rain

embark upon   innovative endeavors
     jolt brain to
          produce fresh neural links

an open mind opens blood vessels

BLOSSOM

I said to the almond tree, Sister, speak to me of God,
and the almond tree blossomed.
—Nikos Kazantzakis

the closest we ever get   to   God
    is not   through study or talk
      belief or prayer or ceremony
        even nature or silence   which come mighty close

    but   through behavior

almond tree does what it does best
      what it does naturally
          it blossoms

same   goal   is   bidden   of   human   saplings

      blossom

LIFE CONSISTS

life consists in   sampling   then saluting
      rarely   solving
          the   mud-splattered   quagmires   of   existence

sun   earthquakes
    justice   travesty
       nomadic zebras   stinging scorpions
        the   sinister and   breathtaking   alike

life consists in not mistaking
     trash clean-up for deep ecology
        puppy dog licks for community
           rousing rhetoric for durable change
    criticism for loathing
       decency for courage
         moaning for love
           stagnation for aging

       life   consists   in   discernment

SKILLFUL SHEDDERS

The wisdom of life consists in the elimination of non-essentials.

—Lin Yutang

the wise ones

declutter

become   skillful shedders

dispersing   worldly attachments

toys   appliances   wardrobe

junk   books

antiques

it's high-time

to

forsake   pointless routines   excessive worry   flurry

nasty manias

sabotaging   grudges

bundles   of   nonsense

dwelling at peace

with what's left

what we have   where we live

who we are

HESED

You're here to love, and be loved, freely.
—ANNE LAMOTT

Hebrew   word   for   "steadfast love"   is   *hesed*
     known by various and sundry embodiments

devotion
     trustworthiness
staying power
     loyalty
allegiance
     fidelity

only   way   for   love   to   sustain   itself
     through   fair or foul   weather

     is   to   grow
      steadfast

GRAYING BUT GRINNING

folks who rate themselves happiest
are often those between 82 and 85

on average
geezers are more relaxed
setbacks aren't the end of our world
quietude and jollity   are considered   partners   not foes
decisions are made more rapidly   unwaveringly
small stuff isn't sweated
unexpected pleasures   pop up
tensions balanced better
practitioners of forbearance

sole caution

elder-joy   remains more   an accomplishment   than a condition

---

PURSUE IT LOVINGLY

There is no solution; therefore, let us pursue it lovingly.
—Harold Mitchell

there is   no   flawless path
swerving
through   life's labyrinth

no conceivable way
to purge
grief
spite
anxiety   slights

whenever   feasible

restart engine   shift   gears

advance   lovingly

CLARITY

Those who are mentally and emotionally healthy are those who have learned when to say yes, when to say no, and when to say whoopee!
—Willard S. Krabill

life   on paper   isn't all that   byzantine

      trickiness raises
        its ugly head
          in the execution

when

      yes   masks as a maybe
        no   is muffled
          whoopee   falls flat

      healthiness   banks upon

        clarity

ONLY IMPERMANENCE LASTS

Look very closely:
only impermanence lasts.
The floating world, too, will pass.
—Ikkyu Sojun (1394-1481)

impermanence   can   either drive   us   to despair
or   vault us   toward   increased mindfulness

we   are   fleeting   creations
constantly   evolving   and   dissolving
unable   to repeat   anything   exactly
or predict   anything   precisely

yet

able   to   live comfortably
confidently
compassionately

inside   each-and-every   ticktock

STRETCHED

"Attention, attention, attention"   wrote   Zen master Ikkyu
centuries ago when pressed to pen highest wisdom attainable

"But what does attention mean?"   hounded   fussy disciple
"Well, attention means attention!"

attention derives from   Latin word *attendere*   meaning "to stretch"

in   authentic   eldering
we are   wholly   spent
our   souls   are   unfailingly   stretched

everything   we   imagine   possess   dread   venture

s-----t-----r-----e-----t-----c-----h-----e-----d

STAY FULLY ALIVE

The glory of God is a human being fully alive.
—Irenaeus of Lyons

it's bad enough to discover Yahweh fuming
and stomping around the celestial haunt
girdled by angels strumming harps
and slothful humans gorging grapes
    heaven is honeyed

God's dismay intensifies
with wafting chorus of interminable halleujahs
    from mortals

"Desist   oh earthlings   be not insipid grovelers
    you were not created to mouth mindless praise
        brown-nosing   for parcels   of everlastingness!
    Rise up   my offspring   stand unbroken
        tango your awe   roar your grievances
            in   full-spirited   measure
                stay fully alive."

FRUITION

I choose to risk my significance,
to live so that which came to me as seed
goes to the next as blossom,
and that which came to me as blossom,
goes on as fruit.
—Dawna Markova

nothing   counts more   during the homestretch

than bringing   our   worthiest dreams
our *dharma* (duty)
to some level of fruition

but it won't happen
if we hole up in cocoons of refuge
or motor with the brakes on

fruition
comes to those

who   risk   their   significance

CUP

sometimes our cup
　　　　is brimming
　　　　　　　even spilling over

　　other times
　　　　filled with mere droplets

　　　　　half-full

　　　　　dry
　or
　　　no　cup　is　locatable

　　　　find one

　　　fashion one

　　　　be one

GO OUT ON A LIMB

Go out on a limb; that's where the fruit is.
—WILL ROGERS

from dawn until dusk

rounding   our final bends

life is essentially   a bunch of   seductive gambles

therefore

without attempting   foolish things

sort out   smart   from   dumb

risks

then   then

snatch   savor

a   clump   of

hanging

fruit

off   the   Tree   of   Life

SOLVITUR AMBULANDO

It is solved by walking.

—Soren Kierkegaard

the time may well arrive

    when we are physically hobbled

       body stricken

      bed-ridden

      immobile

           keep the faith

our mind   may still be able   to circumambulate

       wherever it willeth

EVERYTHING BEAUTIFUL

God has made everything beautiful in its own time.

—ECCLESIASTES 3:11

the Eternal One

has spawned

beauty

in multifarious figures and essences

of animals trees elements

humans as well

each

in our own fashion

beautiful

not as in pretty unruffled glamorous

beautiful as in

downright wondrous

TAKING VOWS SERIOUSLY

The power of a promise is the power to stick
with what we are stuck with.
—Stanley Hauerwas

i've broken   important vows   during my lengthy sojourn
bet you have too

as we traverse   our concluding laps
it's sanguine   to remember

nobody ever quite leaves a previous vow   patterns pieces glom on

vows can often be   repaired or updated

busted vows   need not bust us

radically fresh vows   can be chiseled   upon sunrise

TUNE UP

The first thing a musician must do is tune the instrument.
There is no way a performance can overcome bad tuning.
—DICK BOEKE

during our elective years
we quickly sort out   important   from   petty
from   inconsequential   concerns

determined   to stay   on purpose

tuning up   our assorted possessions   cars and instruments
most of all
tuning up our persons
every dawn

with a body prayer
basic isometrics
examining sacred texts
stroll around the neighborhood
a reassuring chant

whatever ignites our spirit

INTERIOR REALM

Life is just a chance to grow a soul.
—A. POWELL DAVIES

hunting futilely

hither   yon   forwards   backwards

treasure lies within

grave   tussles   transpire   inside

immense resources await

CREDENTIALS OF HUMANITY

I've noticed that the older, the more gnarled the cherry tree, the greater the profusion of blossoms. And sometimes the oldest and dustiest bottles hold the most sparkling wine. I'm drawn to faces lined with crow's feet, those "credentials of humanity," beautifully lit within.

—WILLIAM SLOANE COFFIN

weather-beaten   trees
like humans

can   produce   a lushness of flowering
                          a bursting of fragrance

          yet   truth be told
    not all in our golden years
          are burgeoning

some are withering   others are wracked
      with   malady   misfortune

    our   well-being   banks   on
          heaps   of
                    pluck   and   luck

PEACE AND JOY

Peace is joy at rest;
joy is peace on its feet.
—Veronica Goines

it's   not an   either/or   situation   for   grizzled nomads

we   covet   pursue   both

abundant   peace

sumptuous   joy

settling   for nothing   less

HASTEN SLOWLY

Hasten slowly and ye shall soon arrive.

—MILAREPA

renown   Tibetan   yogi

is   joined

by throngs   of spiritual mentors

encouraging   earthlings

during   life's   third act

to   keep   on   progressing

at   methodical   pace

living   unflappably

unclogged   with   busyness

swift   enough   to   make noticeable strides

deliberate   enough   to   marinate

amidst   the   charitable   juices   of   reality

FORGIVENESS

The stupid neither forgive nor forget; the naive forgive and forget;
the wise forgive, but they do not forget.
—THOMAS SZASZ

above all else

don't   confuse   forgetting   and   forgiving

especially   at   the eleventh-hour

acknowledge   the   harm

you've   delivered   and   received

then

as able

anchor   said   damage and misery   in   yesteryear

close the open wound

clear the air   clean the slate

life flowing   freely   and   forwardly

craves

full-fledged   forgiveness

KOYAANISQATSI

A word in the Hopi language that means living an out-of-kilter, shallow existence, while being called to shape a more balanced, resourceful life.

the goal   of a fulfilled existence   is never   pure length

one can pile up   astounding numbers   while paddling
in the shallows

living longer   for its own sake   is   senseless   vain

dimensions   that matter most   for eldering

breadth—am I   adding   width   scope   expanse to my days?

depth—am I   wrestling with   life's   imponderables?

height—am I   elevating   with gusto   purpose   appreciation?

BOUNTIFUL BLESSING

The power of our blessing is not diminished by illness or age.
Our blessings become even more powerful as we grow older...
surviving the buffeting of our experience.
—RACHEL NAOMI REMEN

as we aspire   to make our farewell trail   a holy one

it's wise to remember that   to bless   means   to mark
or consecrate

                          existence

            in ways   our prehistoric ancestors   did

            sprinkling   life's altars   with blood

our final tour of duty   requires living   with   praise and glee

            infused with   pain   slash   sacrifice

            a   bountiful   blessing

                  may it be so

BOTH/ANDIAN

It is better to light a candle than to curse the darkness,
but there is no harm in doing both.
—Judith Viorst

my friend Jaco
coined the evocative term   "both/andian"
    meaning
            creatures are destined
    to be perennial puzzlers

experiencing sadness even while joyful
    setting boundaries to fortify bonds of affection
            opening up and bolting down concurrently

    bidden to cherish the past
        chart the future
            while celebrating the present

capable   of lighting candles   and cursing darkness
                at the same time

SABBATH

Now weak, short of breath, I find my thoughts drifting to the Sabbath,
the day of rest, and perhaps the seventh day of one's life as well,
when one can feel that one's work is done,
and one may in good conscience,
rest.
—OLIVER SACKS

prone to jam our days
    with wall-to-wall folks
      bulging obligations
        wearing out before our time

rest stops matter
    in travel and music

pauses nourish
    whether eating or making love
    claim   your   quota   of   lulls

      grab   generate   sabbath

MEANING

What is the meaning of life?
There is no meaning.
We bring meaning to it.
—Joseph Campbell

welcome   to our   fate

full-time   sculptors   of   meaning

from   start to   finish

GAMBOL

A merry heart doeth good like a medicine,
but a broken spirit drieth the bones.

—PROVERBS 17:32

during the golden years
   we go a-rummaging
after every magic potion or exercise elixir
     to arrest   inevitable weakening

  gym and spa while healthy locales
    can't deliver bone-deep gratification

   burst open up your trunk
      your chest
      your heart

  join merry-makers union

    gambol

RAKING THE ASHES

A sage is a person who has come to know what is true for him or her,
one who has been refined by the fires of suffering and achieved
a modicum of peace with what they know, believe, and live.
—James Hollis

authentic self-blessing requires   descending deep   within the soul
     we western moderns
  lodge mostly above ground basking in the sunlight
if not limelight—rising   climbing climbing   rising

afternoon constitutes our prime season to chew to brood
  to "rake the ashes" as one versifier puts it
  to "be refined by the fires of suffering"
to confront our ragged and raw shadowed underbelly

    sky-dwellers much of our adult lives
we can we must now   revisit
   the soil from whence we came

   grappling with leftover often unresolved
  angst   anger aloneness   anguish
  severer blessings of the netherworld

THE ESSENCE

I am old age: the essence of life...
—Navajo

the older we get
            not   junior-seniors
but   old-old

the closer we migrate
            toward the crux   of who   we were meant   to be-come

elders   and   crones

    approaching

            our own peculiar   version

                of

                        the essence

STILL

We are the Generosity of Being evolved into human form.
—Brian Swimme

as long   as i'm   still   above ground

and   my body   can budge

i can   make moves

matters   not   if   modest   if minimal

make   jubilation moves

celebrating   the union   of   joy and justice

as long   as i'm   still   awake

my heart   can   be   aroused

SENIOR MATH

The secret to living well and longer is:
eat half, walk double, laugh triple,
and love without measure.
—TIBETAN PROVERB

even though   we've long   since graduated   from formal   grades

calculations   continue

venerables   need to keep   reckoning

Tibetan summation   heralds   maturity

Growing All the Way to Our Grave

SWORD AND CHRYSANTHEMUM

Japanese are both insolent and polite, militaristic and aesthetic;
both sword and chrysanthemum are part of their culture.
—RUTH BENEDICT, 1946

after spending time in Japan
      i would agree with the early post-war
     perspective of this prominent cultural anthropologist

but i would go further

Americans are a living bundle of contradictions
      too

i would go further

aren't   all   humans

living paradoxes

and   always   will   be?

SWEEPERS

If there were no sweepers in the world,
the world would be buried in dust.

—SHABISTARI

Sufi devotees   rightly   urge us
to sweep out   the houses   streets   corners of our cosmos
clearing away muddle   and   debris

call   it   sacred ecology

sometimes
sweeping is   a chore
occasionally   a compulsion   (in my case)
always   an omen   of   sanctified   preservation

creating   barren   spaces
that purify
soul   and   earth

RAISON D'ETRE

Be a lamp, or a life boat, or a ladder.
—RUMI

ways   of   being   for   our   earthly   relations
are
boundless

lamp—light the path
life boat—provide safety net
ladder—furnish rungs

if   none of these three   fit your disposition
find   a   way
create   a   way
your   way

being for others
all entities

is   our   *raison d'etre*

WHAT DOES GOD PRAY?

God studies Torah three hours a day and prays. What does God pray?
"May it be my will that my mercy overcome my anger."
—Rabbi Nachman of Bratslav

god   and   humans frequent   similar crossroads

chiefly   at the latter intervals   of our earthly junket

i'll   speak   for   myself

one   of my   hardest tasks

remains   ridding   my psyche   of crankiness

censure

occasional   bouts of bile

CREATION'S BOUNTY

We do not come into this world. We come out of it,
as leaves from a tree, as the ocean waves,
the universe peoples. Every individual is an expression
of the whole realm of Nature,
a unique action of the total Universe.
—ALAN WATTS

every   life   form

    expressive   munificent

      universal   gift

OUST THE THIEVES

We crucify ourselves between two thieves:
regret for yesterday and fear of tomorrow.
—FULTON OURSLER

remember the past   professing both   failures and coups

await the future   as non-anxiously as possible

live the present   unstintingly

dwell in active   rather than passive   voice

fearlessly   ousting   troublesome   thieves

WHO ARE YOU?

There is at bottom only one problem in the world and this is its name.
How does one break through?
How does one get into the open?
How does one burst the cocoon and become a butterfly?
—THOMAS MANN

seniors   evoke

both   derogatory   labels

and   laudatory   appraisals

which ones will   you   claim?

how will you   exemplify   your   senior years?

carrier of an incurable disease

old fogey

leftover relic

useless drain on society?

untapped   natural   resource

generative

quiet revolutionary

carrier of ancestral understanding?

TENDERLY

Tenderly,
I now touch all things,
knowing one day we will part.
—St. John of the Cross

to   heed   for better   for worse   forever
                deftly   graciously   staunchly

my   beloved's   inner   moods
          and   outer   yearnings

          as   our   golden anniversary   draws nigh

PILGRIM'S GARB

folklorists claim   we need   three bodily trappings

for   jaunt   through life's   rigors and ravages

a sword   a shield   and   sandals

sword for strength   when feebleness strikes

shield for armor   when danger invades

sandals for mobility   when suppleness flags

to   the physical gear   i would append

a   stout   resilient   trunk

when   storms   shake   roots   limbs

FARE FORWARD

Fare forward, travelers! Not escaping from the past into
indifferent lives or into any future...
not to fare well, but to fare forward, voyagers.
—T. S. ELIOT

so tempting

in   our youth-centric   culture

where   "age is the vulture"   (my older brother's phrase)

for seniors to be seduced

into

reversing the clock

rehabbing our persona

wrong direction   fellow voyagers

we   exist not to   go backwards

fare   forward   to   fare   well

OUTWARD BOUND

God is always revising our boundaries outward.
—Douglas Steere

my charge
    my appeal
is
  to live
    intensely and intentionally
my   allotment
        of   days   and   nights

    ever-enlarging   vistas and viewpoints
        agitating   and   lubricating

dousing   self   and   society
    "with liberal sum"
    of
    mellowness
   candor
spontaneity

HARVESTING

Each creature God made must live in its own true nature.
—Mechtild of Magdeburg

it's never too late

to

seed

nurture

bring to fruitfulness

our   harvest

"own true nature"

TIME

I have time.

—WALTER CARRINGTON

spiritual director   reminds   all   pilgrims

specifically seniors   blessed   with the luxury

of a freer   roomier   agenda

to   decelerate

take several breaths

before initiating   any   encounter   action

i have time

you have time

we have time

WHOSE AM I?

Follow the grain in your wood.

—Howard Thurman

my finishing laps

will be   primarily   spent

answering through word and deed

<u>whose</u> am i?

whose <u>am</u> i?

whose am <u>i</u>?

KINSFOLK

We are matter, kindred with ocean and tree and sky.
—Krista Tippett

moseying   amidst

crooked   decaying

flourishing   shuddering

trees

and   knowing   to your   very   stalk   and stem

you are

fellow beings

kinsfolk

HAIKU MIND

A crystalline moment of heightened awareness.
—Patricia Donegan

dwelling   in   moment

focusing   on   here and now

stiffest assignment

AND THE DAY CAME

And the day came when the risk it took
to remain tight in the bud was more painful
than the risk it took to blossom.

—ANAÏS NIN

tightly wound

    veritably sheathed

    the minute arrives

       your   moment

       to   flower

CENTRAL PLEDGE

I strive to be a B+, very good, not perfect mate and mother...
even God said everything was very good.
God is not a perfectionist.
—Rabbi Sherre Hirsch

the   central pledge   to take

upon rising   every   daybreak

is   falling in love   with your own self   anew

even   agreeing to marry

your   self   today

that   good enough   self

the   B+ self

DESPAIR

Despair is not an option.
—Elie Wiesel

actually

despair *is* an option

swallowed daily by legions

of our human household

dare   otherwise

share   otherwise

care   otherwise

FOREST-BATHING

Trees are living creatures—not inert objects merely decorating our world. They live, breathe, eat, sleep, communicate, cooperate, and compete.
—BARRY BOYCE

Thoreau sought to be a *saunterer*   "a holy-lander"
        trekking the soil   leisurely   and   gently

a century later   in Japan   they call it *shinrin-yoku*   or
"forest-bathing"

        wherein
we tense   twitchy   earthlings   consent   to   smell flowers
        rake leaves
            zigzag   unhurriedly

            sopping in nature
                        for

        medicinal   nourishment
                            mystical   camaraderie

SAVORING

wandering   down   the   jagged narrows
of   San Miguel de Allende
i halt   now and again
to catch my breath (altitude: 6500')

to pause
and ponder   the beauteous surrounds

i miss most of   life's cornucopia
have most of my life

today   as a   devouring homestretcher   i relish
smell of   smoking grill
sight of   mushrooming   vegetables
sound of   warbling birds
touch of   sagging branch
taste of   cool agua

AMEN!

grew up   thinking   *Amen*   meant   "so be it"
    merely adding an exclamation point
      to what had just been   spoken or sung

    in truth   it means   "so might it be"
referring not to   an actuality   but   an aspiration

Amen isn't another   sweet   superfluous   four-letter word
    thrown in   for magical measure
      but a promise   to translate   our hopes into deeds
that may heal   and   empower the cosmos
we clasp in common

    Amen!   Amen!   Amen!

A LIGHTER HAND

To be in love is to touch things with a lighter hand.
—Gwendolyn Brooks

caught in culture of clinging vines
squeezed lemons   trapped animals   needless tangles
our souls hunger   for an   endearing stroke

light touches   lift burdens
release   tethered wills
give flight   to   fledglings   and   pensioners alike

love abounds   home and abroad

when   heavy hands   are dropped
flowers   bedded
fuzzy ones   coddled
ribs   tickled
sharp edges   ironed
outcasts   enfolded

love can enter   embattled
embittered zones   and   lighten   all

HUGE

The little things? The little moments? They aren't little.
—Jon Kabat-Zinn

this moment matters

    carrier   of miracles

        treat each   as   present

THE REAL ARTICLE

My faith demands that I do whatever I can, wherever I can,
whenever I can, for as long as I can,
with whatever I have to try to make a difference.
—JIMMY CARTER

any religion   any faith   any   human   enterprise

that challenges   nay demands   that we expend

every ounce   of   energy

during   the entirety   of   our existence

to make   the universe   a   wee bit better

constitutes   the   real article

CONTENT

...for I have learned, in whatever state I am, to be content.
—Philippians 4:11

every thing

brain   heart   limbs   irreversibly age

may   one attitude   reign supreme

during   our   wisdom years

contentedness

WE SHALL NOT BE MOVED

Blessed is the one that trusteth in the Lord,
for they shall be as a tree planted by the waters.

—JEREMIAH 17:7

this biblical passage carries the core of the African-American
gospel hymn *We Shall Not Be Moved*
     popular in civil rights and union movements…with
inspiring refrain
We shall not   we shall not be moved   we shall not
we shall not be moved
     just like a tree   that's planted by the water
     we shall not be moved

during our fading years
     keen judgment   presses us
          to plant ourselves   regularly   near
            flowing rivers

     so we can be   watered   and   replenished
our souls   can germinate
     grow   rock solid   immovable

rooted   for   what is just   beautiful   good

TELEIOS

Act with the authority of your 16 billion years.

—Joanna Macy

biblical term   *teleios* is usually mistranslated   as   "perfection"
when it really means
"abundantly realized"   or   "whole"

i won't reach perfection
neither will you

but to be   abundantly realized   during this one
priceless sojourn
to become   more whole
to act   with   authority
to matter   to the   very end

is   doable   desirable

HAPPINESS

How is it possible to tell people they are all
walking around shining like the sun?
—THOMAS MERTON

we're brainwashed   in our land   to chase joy
        "the pursuit of happiness"   and all   that

when   the truth is
        happiness envelops   us
            abounds
                    it's already here

        nestled
            nurtured   inside   our   beings

SERVANTHOOD

Everybody is created in this universe not for oneself,
but to serve others. That's what we see in Nature.
Everything—grass, fruit, trees, sun, moon, stone, metal—
they're all there to serve others.
Human beings are no exception to that.
—SWAMI SATCHIDANANDA

ultimately   we   find and fulfill   our   vocation

not   through

saving

the cosmos or any of its creatures

but

through   dynamic   tenacious   servanthood

our   finest   final   thank you

DAILIES

*It is only possible to live happily-ever-after
on a daily basis.*
—Margaret Wander Bonanno

aging well

    among other things

       means not waiting around for major moments
          regal   imposing   passages

they'll come   if   they   come

       life is
mainly   a schlep   of monotony
      deadlines   drudgery
delights

      dailies

WABI-SABI

Wabi-sabi is Japanese expression for the beauty of impermanence,
the imperfection of things that are worn and frayed
and chipped through use.
Objects that show their age and use are beautiful.
—Susan Moon

wabi-sabi   rings true

not only   for earthenware   tables   bannisters

woodlands   wildlife

but also   for all   extant   elders and crones

most   assuredly impermanent

downright   imperfect

worn   rough

yet   beautiful

to behold

truly behold

using   spiritual   eyesight

TRANSFIGURATION

Old age either transfigures or fossilizes.
—Marie von Ebner-Eschenbach

give   generously

receive   gratefully   as well

trans-----fig-----ur-----a-----tion

UNIQUE AND PRECIOUS

When you've seen one 81-year-old,

you've seen one 81-year-old.

—T. Franklin Williams

this geriatric specialist   reminds us   of something
we shouldn't   have to be reminded of

every human being   is distinct

and to be treated as such

an emaciated baby   a rebellious teenager
a shiftless mid-lifer   a wobbly senior

major in   the   taxing yet satisfying   labor

of truly engaging
the   unique   and precious   81-year-old
standing in front of you

SENIOR MOMENTS

*I've had a lifetime of junior moments, when one word follows another
in logical and boring succession...a senior moment is a stop sign on the
road of life. It could even be a leg up toward enlightenment.
So I stay calm, let the engine idle, and enjoy the scenery.*
—THICH NHAT HANH

senior moments are

    scorned   as undesirable

       shift   your perspective

         greet   these silly intruders

           as bringers of   sweet   mood   shifts

RESET YOUR MIND

Each day reset your mind to zero, just like your pedometer.

—John Tarrant

as the number of steps

    words

       breaths

          dwindle

   to   a   precious   few

muster breaths   that fill   the air   with joyfulness

     cast words   that   are worthy

         take   steps   that   foster   progress

ELDER

Your heart is a seed. Go plant it in the world.
—SUE KIDD

i hanker not to attain the stature

   of

shaman—wizened link with the spirit world

  tzaddik—"righteous one"

sanyasi—religious ascetic

 bodhisattva—assisting one and all in the quest for enlightenment

  an embodied elder will suffice

incarnating myself precisely where i'm planted

(as the *elder* tree does with its purple berries)

BED OF WOESES

every   senior

  inhabits   a plush garden

    loaded   with   woeses

JOYS OVER JOBS

None are so old as those who have outlived enthusiasm.
—Henry David Thoreau

during the homestretch
operate
mainly
from choices more than duties
joys over jobs

become   inner-directed

it's   the season
your   very   own   season

to major   in   heartfelt   longings

to become   a quickener   rather than   a deadener

FAITHIFY

Faith is the beginning of all good things.

—Buddha

we need   a   launcher

neither   fear   nor   distrust   work

faith   flings   us   forward

LUCKY BOY

Bless us to usefulness.
—DALAI LAMA

only   one of 8,000   buried Terra Cotta warriors   survived
intact
          undamaged   from the 221 B.C.   regime of Emperor Qin
                    upon discovery in 1974
          he was a kneeling archer   nick-named   "lucky boy"

          bought   small replicas   for two   young   grandsons
    in prayerful hope   that they might   become   lucky boys
                    blessed to   survive
                    life's
fierce   constraints   battles   corrosion   plundering

      relatively unharmed
              ever useful
                    mature men
                    kneeling   in service
                          of their   chosen mission

TIME TO DANCE

I never carry a grudge. While you're carrying a grudge,
they're out dancing.
—Buddy Hackett

drop   weighty   luggage

complaining   rancor   envy

join   amazing   dance

SPIRITUAL ALZHEIMERS

Avoid spiritual Alzheimers: the incremental loss of the ability to be grateful and joyful about the daily gifts of life, no matter what the circumstances of our lives are at that moment.

—Louise Penny

seniors   fixate   upon bodily   decline

heed   eroding   mental capacity

while   forgetting   to stem   the tide

of potential   oft   progressive

spiritual   lapses

losing track   of   beauty   humility   ardor

IMPROVEMENT

You are perfect as you are, and you could stand some improvement.
—Suzuki Roshi

you mean   we've proceeded   this far

into   our   sundowner   laps

and   some eccentric   throws   Zen darts

at codgers?

yes

even now

at this   belated stage

there are   adjustments   to be made

our minutes   could   stand   amendments

HOMESTRETCH PRIORITIES

Walk joyfully on the earth
and respond to that of God in every human being.
—GEORGE FOX

practicing   these two   Quaker imperatives

will keep   twilighters   spiritually fit

sauntering   cheerfully   on home

affirming   god-ness   in all

certifies

soulful   progression

BORN OF THE SPIRIT

The wind blows wherever it pleases;
you hear its sound, but you cannot tell
where it comes from or where it is going.
That is how it is with all who are born of the Spirit.

—JOHN 3:8-9

can't imagine   a finer self   to occupy

during eldering epoch

than being   "born of the Spirit"

an   unconstrained

mighty   wind

sailing   freely   onward

GIVE THANKS

…give thanks in all circumstances.
—I Thessalonians 5:18

discoverable

in every   environs

even   debacles

chance   to be appreciative

you   never   miss mark   with thanks

SWIMMING TO SHORE

Lao-tzu   was   allegedly   born   around   604 B.C.
conceived   when his mother   admired   a falling star
    maturing   in her womb   for 62 years

arrived   with a long white beard   and   much wisdom
    his name means   Old Boy
        which is   what i am   as   i write   this poem

an old boy

may   we old boys   and   old girls

    swim   to   shore
neither   paddling furiously   nor   drifting frivolously
    but flowing
        naturally
            easily
                like water

Growing All the Way to Our Grave

MOVING

Sit, walk, or run, but don't wobble.
—Unmon (10ᵀᴴ century Zen Master)

spiders flail spindly legs to the four winds
programmed to march straightforwardly
humans diversify repertoire of moves
by mimicking multi-legged kin

moving *backwards*   in time to perform
tardy emotional excavation

moving *sideways*   that others might shine in foreground

moving *ahead*   in chase of haunting dreams

moving *beneath*   the surface
sleuthing hidden treasures

moving   *in place*
body still   spirit astir

INTO THE WOODS

Being in nature allows the prefrontal cortex to rest and recover,
like an overused muscle.
—FLORENCE WILLIAMS

one of the   sure-fire   remedies

        for   drooping body   and   slumped spirit

are regular treks   into nearby parks

      daytrips   out of town

        strolls in   woody glens

    spending deep time   in countryside

       beholding

       sister lakes

     squeezing   brother trees

   we evolved   straightway   from nature

keep   revisiting   reveling   in our   earthly   roots

CIVILIZATION

my   Japanese and Chinese   are non-existent
   my   Español   sucks
      worse   than   my antiquated   Deutsch

whenever   a human encounter   occurs
            in Mexico
      my esteem quavers
            my voice mumbles

then   from deep within   a *gracias*   or *hola*
            sounds   forth

   and   civilization endures

            momentarily

ROSH HASHANAH

Jewish New Year

blowing of the *shofar*   launches   ten days of penitence

reminding   all   homestretchers

to take stock   reset our spirits

hourly   not just   annually

bring   identity and vision   into closer alignment

engage in   soul-searching   without breast-beating

it's never too late to   repent   reconcile   restore

plot   and   plod   toward

our better   not bitter   selves

AN ANGEL IN THAT ROCK

I saw the angel in the marble and carved until I set it free.
—MICHELANGELO

the eleventh hour   nudges

         the angel   you are

                  the angel   i am

    to be   adroitly sculpted

from   the   boulders of existence

GRIEF

We don't do grief.
—Joan Didion

taboo after taboo   topples
but   grieving well   remains   an American obstacle

comparisons are odious
cease the sweet talk or saccharine prayers
teddy bears only   cart   so much fluff
in face of   the   unbearable

Gref comes from Middle English
meaning   "heavy"   and it is
grief is   weight   robbery   loss   mourning
it cannot be normalized   light-heartened   away

only companioned

ENORMOUS PRIVILEGE

It is an enormous privilege and adventure
to have been a sentient being
on this beautiful planet.
—OLIVER SACKS

take not for granted

hallowed   lifelong excursion

we   are   miracles

HOLINESS HOLDS FORTH

Every day is a god and holiness holds forth in time.
—Annie Dillard

day   arrives   as gift

       but   we can   add to   subtract

            from   its godliness

DEEP TIME

I suffer from a condition that Zen calls FOMS Syndrome—"fear of missing something." It's a form of greed, the urge to cram as many interesting activities into the day as possible...Aging is giving me back the present moment, a better chance to enter deep time.
—SUSAN MOON

most   elders and crones
        if   completely   honest
suffer   from   regular bouts   with FOMS
our time   is more limited   slithering away

so we   feverishly   rush   to fill   our days   and   nights
     rather than   slowly but surely *fulfill* them

   stop racing around
     turn up the quiet
       pay your inner castle   a   profitable   call

       enter   deep   time

RE-FINEMENT

We start fine. Then we got defined. Now we need to get re-fined.
—Swami Satchidananda

in   our sunset season

we've enlisted   the support   of the   Refiner's Fire

burning away   life's unnecessary   superfluous   rubbish

we   are   our own   bosses

in charge

self-governing   at last

we can

finish   our   own   sentences

LAUGHERS LAST

You know you're getting old when you stoop
to tie your shoelace and wonder
what else you can do while you're down there.
—GEORGE BURNS

lest these   poetic pieces   appear too solemn

slightly   burdensome

pause
and   concede

the   limitless   humor   in the odyssey of every senior

be we   bending   rending   fending   mending

we can   we must   poke fun   at our condition
without   one iota   of   self-denigration

"hearty laughter   is a good way   to jog internally…"

expressly for   oldsters

BE A BLESSING

Be a blessing to all the families of the earth.

—GENESIS 12:3

expand   thy circle

all clans   human   animal

summon   our blessing

AMATEUR

One's own self is well hidden from one's own self:
of all mines of treasure, one's own is the last to be dug up.
—Friedrich Nietzsche

you've advanced from   your   day-time   profession
    into   sphere   of full-time   amateurism

      amateur   is   considered pejorative
  but   a dabbler   a hobbyist
yet   when   the concept was born   centuries ago
it connoted   a deep-digger   a lover of something
one   who adored   an endeavor   then
passionately pursued it

time   to find   your   sweet   spot   "one's own self"
        time   to stride forth
               time   to become a bona fide

amateur

SILENTLY DRAWN

Let yourself be silently drawn by the strange pull
of what you really love. It will not lead you astray.

—Rumi

at this later hour

    stream   noiselessly   amidst brook

        of   your real   passion

RESTLESSNESS

There is a restlessness in my soul that I've never conquered,
not with motion, marriages, or meaning. It's still there.
—Merle Haggard

as   we twilighters   advance

there   routinely   persist   butterflies   in the stomach

disquieting thoughts

agitated flashes

edginess

FRENZIED INTERPLAY

Just remember, we're all in this alone.

—Lily Tomlin

we come   into this universe   alone
                        emerging from the womb
bare   yelping as we burst   from sheltered solitude
        squarely   into   exposed   blaring scene

                we also   exit alone

even   the interlude
      (whether   painful   loving   boring   happy
                   or   a   zany mixture)
           finds   us   incurably   alone

our   existential condition   is   aloneness
    our   essential call   is   community

      our fate   is   a   frenzied   interplay
             between the two

ALIGNMENT

At age 15 I set my intention upon studying; at 30 I established myself in society; at 40 I freed myself of delusions; at 50 I understood the mandates of Heaven; at 60, I could hear with clarity; and at age 70 what my heart desired and what was right came into alignment.
—CONFUCIUS (551-479 BC)

planetary one

bold shaper of history

lover of wisdom

may we sprout in alignment

at our comparable ages

MATES

In poems, joy and sorrow are mates.
They lie down together, their hands
all over each other...
—ELLEN BASS

joy and sorrow are braided

into the warp and woof

of   aging

moments   of   pure exhilaration   exist

moments   of   deep-seated sadness   arise

harvest time

charges us   to "participate joyfully in the sorrows of the world"

to use the mythologist's   dramatic   phrase

Crown Jewels

*There's nothing like a ninety-three-year-old at an antiracism rally
to bring tears to everyone's eyes. Be that person.*

—Sparrow

surveying   oldest   continuous civilization

China

where   ageless riches   lie

and   ancestor worship thrives

a neighboring truth emerges

never to be forgotten

elders   crones   everywhere

are   "crown   jewels"

as well

GO WITH ALL YOUR HEART

Wherever you go, go with all your heart.

—Confucius

whether traveling at home or abroad
    internally   externally   eternally

go
clear-hearted
    brave-hearted
        open-hearted
           tender-hearted

journey
with
    "all your heart"

AMOR

Life begins with love, is maintained with love, and ends with love.
—Tsokayi Rinpoche

it's   no   accident   that the word
amor   (love)
is   scrupulously close to the Greek word
amusso   (choke)

we spend   our entire lives   trying   to embody
the distinction

tracking   healthy bonds   where   we attach rather than
suffocate

at   the   tail end

still trying to   wrap up   our   primary   ties

in ways   that   will   enhance
rather than   stifle
the   Spirit

MAO

I am human. Nothing human is alien to me.
—TERENCE (195-159) BC

Chinese dictator   Chairman Mao Tse-Tung   administered
nearly   3 decades   of   tyranny

a   malevolent   despot   who wrecked   everything   ancient and
traditional
a   perpetrator   of   gross abuses   and   incalculable deaths

yet as with us all
upon deeper delving

Mao was   an acknowledged theorist   military strategist
competent poet
long-awaited visionary   who drove imperialism   out of China
revered by   millions of Chinese   still today
his mug   plastered everywhere   across   this   gigantic   landmass

may we remember
the worst   among us   contain shards   of
creative goodness
the best   among us   can engender
unthinkable   fiendishness

OUR BEST SEASON

Spring flowers and autumn moon,
summer breeze and winter snow.
An unemcumbered mind
is our best season.
—HUIKAI (1183-1260)

it is neither too early

nor too late

to   taper

our surplus burdens

and weighty encumbrances

unclutter   the mind
            unwrinkle   the soul

A HEART LIKE THAT TREE

There is a tree before the gate
where birds nest and fly,
unbidden and unmissed.
To have a heart like that tree,
would not offend the way.
—JUDUN (825-923)

during the hours   that remain   on my finite calendar
may   i possess   the   heart   of a   tree
that welcomes   birds   of   variant stripes and feathers
nesting   upon   its boughs

may   i receive   whatever   millstones and boons   come
my way

extending   friendly   limbs

RESILIENCE

The bamboo grows one node at a time,
it bends in the storm but springs back.
Its character radiates from an open heart, and its strength
rises from running roots entwined with others.
—Deng Ming-Dao

keep bounce   stay springy

    supple   buoyant   to the end

    crucial   senior trait

VOTING

Every aspect of our lives is in a sense a vote
for the kind of world we want to live in.
—FRANCES LAPPE MOORE

ballot box opens at dawn
without fail
in villages everywhere

at sunset's close
results are tallied
for welfare and roads
schools and taxes
plus sundry
candidates   measures

voting   occurs   every day
             charging   languid   seniors

to   weigh citizenship
                assess   relationships
                mold   earth's well-being

LET THERE BE LIGHT

There's a crack in everything,
That's how the light gets in.
—Leonard Cohen

as   darkness   falls

our   physical   mental   relational   cracks

magnify

fear not   freeze not

keep grinding

remain resourceful

disciplined

contributor

light will emerge

OBEDIENCE

*Satan disguises as an angel of light. So it is not strange
if humans disguise ourselves as servants of righteousness.*
—II Corinthians 11:1-15

supreme virtue of Confucianism is obedience

value of   well-cultivated humans

displaying   familial piety

respectable allegiance   to homeland   and neighbors

yet   beware of self-righteous folks

whose virtues   imperceptibly glide   into vices

emperors become dictators

country's principles are compromised

parents turn abusive

religion shrinks into bromides

hearts calcify

during   our concluding   days and nights   on earth

may   we grow obedient   only   to the   worthiest dictates

of our   own   consciences

to the   invitations   and   injunctions

of   Love

MY WHOLE SWORD

Foible originally meant the weak part of a sword,
while forte refers to the sword.
—BARBARA ROHDE

as   i forge   the   remaining breadth   of my journey

i wish   to utilize   the   entirety   of   my rapier
        every weakness   every strength

        acknowledging   flaws and infirmities
    as well as flexing   muscles and assets

        i desire   to draw   my whole sword
                    in every
                outstanding   life-skirmish

WE ARE WHAT WE ARE

Though much is taken, much abides, and though
we are not now that strength which in old days
moved earth and heaven, that which we are, we are.
—A<small>LFRED</small> N<small>ORTH</small> T<small>ENNYSON</small>

one   of the secrets   to   well-crafted   aging
is making peace
(not absolute   but   adequate   peace)

with   our current   location
condition
identity
track   record

gleaning lessons   from   waning strength

SEVENTH GENERATION

We always keep in mind the Seventh Generation to come.
It's our job to see that the people coming ahead,
the generations still unborn, have a world no worse than ours—
and hopefully better.

—Oren Lyons, known as the Onondaga Faithkeeper

although the number of   moves and decrees
are shrinking   as we grow   long-in-the-tooth

decisions   remain ever precious
maybe more precious

and   oh   so   germane
to the well-being of those not yet here

live today   as if we're   preparing the way
for
the seventh generation

because   we   are

CONSCIOUS AGING

I will do what I can, with what I have,
in the time that I have, in the place that I am.
—Ruby Abraham

conscious aging may not produce more years

only more depth and thickness

to the years we receive

conscious aging means   seeking   moral fluency

ensouling   what   i   know to be true

cherishing   forest-fresh   excursions

extracting   life's   ample   nectars

IT GOES ON

In three words, I can sum up everything
I've learned about life.
It goes on.
—Robert Frost

debacles   occur

    delights   enticements   arise

      dictum   it goes on

TO KNOW GOD

To know God is to do justice.

—JEREMIAH 22:13-16

we spend   an   entire lifetime
raising   wrongheaded   questions
who is God?   *what* is God?

when the   useful inquiries remain: *where* is God?   *when* is God?

we learn   no matter   how   weather-worn

we come closest to the Eternal

when we are   most humane
assisting the fallen   healing the broken

being human   nearing god

EQUANIMITY

Zen master: "On bad days I'm okay.
On good days, I'm also okay.
This is called equanimity."

key   vibrant   virtue

during   this   quake/creak   called aging

e—qua—nim—i—ty

FACE

You shall rise up before the hoary head,
and honor the face of an older person…
—LEVITICUS 19:32

rooted in Chinese culture
　　　　is *tiu lien* ("losing face")
fear of suffering public shame
　　　　　　preserve appearance of decorum at all costs

　　　　yet　　at this leg　　in　　my marathon

　　　i don't want to　　　save my face　　　just disclose it

i desire　to greet　my　remaining　　hours
　　　　with a genuine　honorable　face
　　　　that can be met head-on
　　　　　whether　　smiling or fuming

one that　　reveals　　rather than veils　　my substance

SPANIELING

The afternoon knows what the morning never suspected.
—Swedish proverb

sometimes the best way to spend the   afternoon of life

is to turn   into   a   spaniel

the breed   with broad muzzle
                dense   wavy   fur
                        droopy ears

mooching   over to a favorite corner

lying back
curling up
rolling over

spanieling

PARENTING

Making the decision to have a child is momentous.
It is to decide forever to have your heart go walking
around outside your body.
—Elizabeth Stone

unquestionably one of the   roughest   toughest   vocations   of all

sometimes successful   occasionally disastrous   always   grueling

releasing   our   offspring   to the world

then   relinquishing   them   utterly

upon   our closing   gasp

parental love   is often   *pained-love*   as the Chinese say

since   we are the roots   giving birth   to the branches

but   as the sap   invariably rises

it doesn't   always   descend

DEEP LISTENING

as we rumble   and   ramble   homeward

deep listening   is   paramount

listening   to   and   with every   last fiber   of our   being

heeding   the body   mind   soul
                    of the   creation
                        and all its inhabitants

embodying   the Japanese ideogram   comprised of 3 figures

ear   eye   heart

THY MIGHT

Whatsoever thy hand findeth to do, do it with thy might.

—Ecclesiastes 9:10

as long as our limbs aren't frozen
as long as our hands bend

they remain gifts of creation

to   be   sourced

manipulating   objects
massaging   backs
tending   earth

every morning you roll out of bed

translate   thy might   in   thy head

through   thy heart

via   thine hands

AT 80

At 20, we worry what others think about us,
at 40 we don't care what others think about us,
and at 60 we discover that they haven't been thinking
about us much at all.
—BOB HOPE

then   turning eighty

   we fulfill   own   destiny

      freed   to complete   life

DIRT

Of all the paths you take in life,
make sure a few of them are dirt.
—JOHN MUIR

sprouting   from the dirt

while alive   pound turf   often

hailing   muddy   home

Growing All the Way to Our Grave

DOSE

our word   dose   arrives   from the Greek *dosis*   meaning gift

a modest amount   of medicine

during   the rough patches   of   later life

we would   do well   to furnish   sisters and   brothers

with   comforting   prescriptions

from the cupboard of our heart

for   healing   not   curing

REMAIN VULNERABLE

Whatever you do, don't shut off your pain;
accept your pain and remain vulnerable,
because it is trying to hand you a priceless gift:
the chance of discovering what lies beyond sorrow.
—SOGYAL RINPOCHE

from   youngster-hood   throughout   mid-life

we ardently   aspire to appear   formidable   unassailable

steering clear   whenever possible   of   painfulness

now

navigating   the   elder threshold

it's time to relax our defenses   open   up   to heartache

awaken   to   the   gracious   gifts-within-sorrow

remaining   vulnerable

LARGER LIFE

And then the knowledge comes to me that I have space
within me, for a second, timeless, larger life.
—RAINER MARIA RILKE

paradox of paradoxes

as we age

certain horizons   narrow   shrivel

as other   spheres   intensify   bulge

especially

an   inner universe

wherein   homestretchers   can   heartily explore

"a second, timeless, larger life"

DAUER IM WECHSELN

What abides amidst change.

—Goethe's personal motto

through   the raw   oft-blistering

labyrinth of aging

Goethe's   challenge   haunts

dauer   im   wechseln?

dauer   im   wechseln!

what are   the durables   of   your journey

what sustains you through   cold lonely nights
scorching steamy days

what   steadies and grounds   your organism?

EROS

When I can no longer love you in any way whatsoever,
please consider me dead.
—Ashleigh Brilliant

in Greek mythology   Eros appears   as one of the   four original gods

alongside   Chaos   Gaia   Tartarus

Eros   supplies   life-enhancing   juice   all our days and nights

Eros   personifies   the irrepressible   yearning

to create   connect   caress

never lose sight of

never lose touch with

this

august   deity

NEVER TOO LATE

They who are without sin among us, let them throw a stone at her first.
—JOHN 8:7

in 1937   the Nanjing Massacre   occurred
          300,000 civilians killed   80,000 women raped

                    openly denied
        downplayed   at best
            by   the perpetrating   Japanese

          yet beware of   casting blame   abroad
without acknowledging   the blunders and brutalities of
      our own country
              enslaving Africans   Native American genocide

        never too late   to acknowledge   our most grievous deeds
    and atone   for   intractable sins   both   public and personal

              never too late to use
              the rocks in our hands
                    to make some stone soup

SOUL SHINES THROUGH

It is only with the Heart that one can see rightly;
what is essential is invisible to the eye.
—Antoine de Saint-Exupery

an unpreventable   incurable   progressive   brain disease

Americans   fear   Alzheimers   more than   dying

however   never forget this

an   ailing   person
is no empty shell
but fortified with soul

even when   you   are not recognized
you know who they are

even when   they   cannot speak
they possess receptors

while breathing   every   one   inhabits   a   "life-world"

beneath   beyond cognition

love   can always   be felt

MID-DAY SNOOZE

I stretch out both legs and take a long nap; and here there is neither true nor false. Truly, such is the essence of the Way.
—CHINESE ZEN MASTER

the basic push   of   our   adult   years

is   being effective   and   efficient
acquiring   achieving

until   we grow   hoarier

bushed   worn-out

decelerating   braking   stopping
time to rest   with zest

catching   a   long   glorious   nap

where   no deals   are   negotiated

no truths   captured

no   apparent   advancement

yet   upon   rising   fully   restored

GENERATIONAL BRIDGE

If we do not initiate the young, they will burn down
the village to feel the heat.
—African proverb

our culture is   initiation-starved

youngers   ravenous   to obtain an identity
take to the streets

drawn to   depression   drugs   violence

elders arise   elders arise   elders arise
you're still on duty

find a youth   blood or not

to-buddy-and-be-buddied-by

before you die

build   a   long-lasting   generational   bridge
and walk it   with   youngers
plank by plank
until   you   can   no longer
walk

BAD NEWS…GOOD NEWS

The bad news is time flies.
The good news is you're the pilot.
—Michael Altshuler

as   our days   and   nights   zoom   along

the universe   invites

nay   urges

us

to be passengers   every now and then

but   mainly

to climb   into   the cockpit

harness up

master   the controls

become   aviators

take flight

THE SEEING EYE

Seeing is a born faculty; knowing is acquired.
To see is to go direct to the core.
The seeing eye of Japan is the perception of significant loveliness…
—Yanagi Soetsu (1889-1961),
founder of Mingei (folkcraft) movement in Japan

all my life   i have been hungry for definite meanings
   descriptive labels
     definitive analysis

     now   in my waning days i aspire to experience
         with the seeing eye and unsullied soul

      a painting
       a crisis
         a fellow creature
         a forest

life in all   of its   wondrous   complexity
         more   immediately   intuitively

FEW DESIRES

Manifest plainness, embrace simplicity,
reduce selfishness, have few desires.
—LAO TZU

as   our   hours   ebb   and   flow   with   the
receding tide

so   will our   cravings   pursuits

maximize   by   minimizing

full life   few desires

i desire   my body and spirit   to grow
                                                in deeper congruence

i desire   to pass on or toss out   personal   effects

   i desire   to benefit   the universe   and all its tenants

---

CARING CO-CREATORS

*Like Abraham, who at 75 years of age, sought a vision, elders should
look out and respond to the life that still needs to be protected,
affirmed, dignified…and become caring co-creators of this universe.*
—WILLIAM SLOANE COFFIN

our   moral duties   aren't terminated   when we reach 75

we're   still bona fide   sentinels

majoring   in   ethics

slough not   slumber not

join   other sisters and brothers

alongside   the Infinite One

in protecting   affirming   dignifying

our lone   quivering   cosmos

GOOD DAY

Every day is a good day.
—Yunmen Wenyan (864-949 CE)

naturally

bad alternatives   lurk

bad things   occur

bad conditions   must be combated

nonetheless

good never disappears

good sticks around

good permeates

every   24-hour-period

GRAVITAS

core   Roman   virtue

conveys   rock-hard   dignity

way of eldering

A COURAGEOUS HOSPITALITY

May you find in yourself
a courageous hospitality
towards what is difficult,
painful and unknown.
—JOHN O'DONOHUE

life's   losses   mount

saddled with   surrounded by

ghastly   ailments

untimely   tragedies

torment   sears itself   into our   husk

as our strength   buoyancy wane

the   boldest and bravest   response   we can rally
is   unearthing

then exhibiting

a   courageous   hospitality

EMPTY HUTS

Do I take delight in empty huts?
—Anguttara Nikaya 10:48

monks and nuns   meditate   in   empty huts

every   elder and crone   is charged

to occupy   the equivalent   of   an empty hut

spaces within   or without   the home

where we sit   regularly   solo   undisturbed

soaking   strengthening

our

soul

EMOTIONAL ECHOES

Walk into nature with your emotional not with your intellectual self.
Open wide your heart so that you can become moist and drink deeply
from the emotional echoes that you receive from the frown
of a gnarled tree or the twist of a branch.
—Malidoma Some

more than   machines or ideologies   earth   itself
from soil to sky

    has nurtured   our very nature   from   birth   onward

    as conscious seniors   it's   the season   to revisit   outdoors

            expressing   our undying   gratitude

                        through

capering   amidst   rivers   animals   trees

        opening our hearts

                    becoming moist

                            drinking deeply

        all   the way   to   our   earthly   chambers

HEAVEN

We speak of going to heaven, as if we could be made happy solely
by being put in a happy place. But the true heaven, the only heaven
that Jesus knew is a state of the soul. It is inward goodness. It is the love
of God in the heart, going out into our life and character.
—JAMES FREEMAN CLARKE, 19ᵀᴴ CENTURY MINISTER

why wait around for   heaven

a   promised-land

some bye-and-bye

find heaven

be heaven   while   gallivanting   around

on earthly soil

and   if you need   to employ   map-quest

the   main route   lies

through   "inward goodness"

"love of God in the heart"

HOLY WASTE

Then Mary took a pound of expensive ointment, made of pure nard,
and anointed Jesus' feet and wiped them with her hair.
The house was filled with the fragrance of the perfume.

—JOHN 12:3

may   we grow   bolder as   we grow   older

refusing   to be   acrimonious   or   parsimonious

gladly   pouring forth   costly ointments

from   the   cupboards   of   our soul

anointing   the   cosmos   and   all   its   creatures

being a   spendthrift   for   justice-and-joy

unleashing   a

delightful   fragrance

pleasing the Nazarene

with our holy waste

TONGLEN

You take it all in. You let the pain of the world
touch your heart and you turn it into compassion.
—GYALWA KARMAPA

tonglen   is the   Tibetan Buddhist   practice

where we   intentionally

breathe in   suffering

breathe out   comfort

abetting   ourselves   others   all sentient beings

instead   of stuffing   flushing distress   as is   our wont to do

embrace anguish
take it in
transform it

PROMISES AND MILES

The woods are lovely, dark and deep,
But I have promises to keep,
And miles to go before I sleep,
And miles to go before I sleep.
—Robert Frost (1874-1963)

bard   known for   colloquial   realistic   language
musical rhymes

nestled   close to   the heartbeat   of the   ordinary pilgrim

Frost   composed   this poem   before   reaching   fifty-years-old

my   remaining miles   aren't   as   plentiful

but   amply   sufficient

to   fulfill   the major

promises   i   still   wish   to   keep

in   the   dark   deep   woods

before   enjoying my   final   sleep

TOUCHING

When we grow older, our sense of touch degrades.
—TIFFANY FIELD

the nerve endings   of every elder and crone   hunger
for tactile nourishment

touch remains   until our dying day
our largest sense   our most social organ
our mandatory medicine

so   go   forth   and   find   an object   animal   tree   human

to touch and be touched by

today

SMILING

Waking up this morning, I smile.
Twenty-four brand new hours are before me.
I vow to live fully in each moment
and to look at all beings with eyes of compassion.
—CHAN PHAP DANG

what more   conscious   way

to launch   every   morn   than

radiating   warmth

TEARS

in 1942   my government   incarcerated   all Japanese

on the West Coast...   2/3 were   US citizens

including   our own   Sue Masanaga   housekeeper
                    nanny   family

no one intervened   as she was hauled   off to   internment camp

i   was a little baby   watching the tears   flow   down my
Dad's brown face

        75 years later   i make   a pilgrimage   to Japan

                Sue's other homeland
to immerse myself   in   cultural   legacy   artistic   treasures
            to compose   death   poems
                to wipe

a few   still wet tears   (sobbing)

                and   to   heal   still   gritty tears   (gashes)

        of   racial remorse

STILLNESS

When you look at a tree and perceive its stillness,
you become still yourself.
Stillness is where creativity and solutions to problems are found.
—ECKHART TOLLE

stillness   premier   trait

throughout   entire biosphere

humanity   too

COUNTERING COWARDICE

The human race is a race of cowards.
I am not only marching in the parade,
I am carrying a banner.
—Mark Twain

spells of   cowardice   pop up and   plague   humanity

all our days and nights

our job remains   relentlessly   to oppose   spinelessness

to be   intrepid   audacious   gutsy

keep on marching   in   the   parades of righteousness

keep on carrying   bold   colorful   expressive banners

keep on resembling   what   each   placard   shouts

keep on   keeping on

sanctifying our homestretch

A LOVE BREATH

There is a way of breathing
that's a shame and a suffocation.
And there's another way of expiring,
a love breath, that lets you open infinitely.
—RUMI (1207-1273)

in our   wiser moments   seniors   heed   the astuteness
of   the Persian   Sunni   Muslim   jurist   scholar   poet

expiring   breathing out

yea   living-and-dying

daily

one   love breath   after   another

opening   infinitely

DOUBLE SONG

Life is saying the long good-bye and learning to say it
gracefully, holding on and letting go amidst what
novelist Wallace Stegner would call,
"My unbroken double song of love and lamentation."
—KIM HEACOX

ambivalence   peppers

    entire   earthly   excursion

we're   fated

            to   harbor   mixed emotions

            dance on   the   razor's edge

            wrestle mightily

with   reality's

        double song

    of love   and   lamentation

QUAN YIN

Buddhist goddess of compassion

"who hears the cries of the world"

even when   our frame   is   aching

      our neighborhood   clashing

          our earth   degrading

             our climate changing

    do not despair

      do not go numb

        do not use age as an apology

      pay homage to Quan Yin

absorb the suffering

   soothe the sting

    bridge the chasms

    answer the cries

   with   a robust yield

       of

          dogged justice

tender mercy

DECREPITUDE

Every breath, new chances.
—Buddhist saying

even   the word itself   sounds   creaky   feeble   hapless

we will   physically   erode   and   tatter   over   time

but   decrepitude   is   mainly   due   to   wanton   neglect

a   preventable   spiritual   malady

by   staying   as   vigorous   as   feasible

sharing   our   knacks

proving   valuable

sprouting

WONDERMENT

*One of the realities we're all called to go through is to move
from repulsion to compassion and from compassion to wonderment.*
—Mother Teresa

in our ceaseless   oft-futile   labors   to make the world
a trace   lovelier   and more just

we   confront folks   situations

that   spread   malice   cruelty

fortunately

with immense   stamina   openheartedness

every now and again   we   can   evolve

from repulsion

to   compassion

to   wonderment

FACING FEAR

When asked how he related with fear,
the Zen master Kobun Chino Roshi remarked:
I agree. I agree.

during   elderhood   fears   customarily   escalate

fear of getting sick   or sicker
            fear of falling
                fear of losing   hearing   eyesight   control
                        license   mind   mate
                    fear   of dying   poorly

        counsel   from   sages   over   the   ages

            don't flee fear

            don't fight fear

                face it
                            befriend it

            whenever   you   can

SUPREME TRUTH

*We do not have solitary, isolated creatures. It is beyond our
imagination to conceive of a single form of life that exists alone
and independent, unattached to other forms.*
—LEWIS THOMAS

connectedness   is the   chief   inescapable   truth   of existence
confirmed   by science   and   religion alike

the universe   bespeaks   bedrock   kinship
every   entity   living on earth   is composed of   the   same stuff

golden   geezers

relish

final   season

of

praising   weeping   dancing   serving

alongside   another human   a god   an animal   a tree

live   interdependently

CHARACTER

*Aging is no accident; it is necessary to the human condition,
intended by the soul. Our last years confirm and fulfill character.*
—James Hillman

kharakter   according to   Greek origins

denotes

making   sharp   indelible   marks

upon life's tablet

imaginative   conscious aging   carves

astute   engravings

character

LONG ENOUGH

Life is too short to be little.

—Benjamin Disraeli

cease being puny

miserly   stingy   of   self

your   singular   life

is plenty long   long   enough

for   unleashing   lavish   love

THINK ON THESE THINGS

Whatsoever things are true, whatsoever things are honest,
whatsoever things are just, whatsoever things are pure,
whatsoever things are lovely, whatsoever things are of good report…
think on these things.
—PHILIPPIANS 4:8

Paul and Timothy   deliver   sound doctrine   to Philippi
in Greece

        way back   in 49 AD

relevant   for   those   of us   playing   "the back nine"   of life

    ponder   deeply   these   noble virtues

    internalize

    incarnate

    their   force

INTEGRITY

*Jack pines are not limber trees and won't win many beauty contests
either. But this valiant old tree, solitary in its silence, speaks of
wholeness, an integrity that comes from being what you are.*
—DOUGLAS WOOD

following   the   example   of this earthly kin

it's   our era   to quit vying   for plaques   or   make-overs

agreeing   to become the person   we were created to be

Jack and Jill   pines   on   lonesome   rocky mountains

baring

"strength   of character   and   perseverance
survival of wind   drought   cold   heat   disease…"

GUIDE FROM BEYOND

Every morning a new arrival.
A joy, a depression, a meanness…as an unexpected visitor.
Be grateful for whoever comes
because each has been sent
as a guide from beyond.
—Jalaluddin Rumi

we think we've experienced it all

as well-honed seniors

then life   delivers   surprises

even   shocks

welcome each   new arrival

whatever the guise   whatever the message

as something   someone

that   keeps us   growing

all the way to the grave

Mindful Dying

In truth, everything arises in order to disappear;
everything we have, everything we think we are,
must at some point be surrendered,
for it is only on loan from the bounty of the Divine.
—ALISTAIR SHEARER

FACT

World death rate is holding steady at 100%.
—WORLD HEALTH ORGANIZATION

no matter whether we believe in heaven

reincarnation of body

immortality of soul

continuity of consciousness

or   ongoing evolution
of

god knows what?

death poses and delivers   a   decisive thump

closure   to our   physical   corporeal

this-earthly-existence

thud

ANSWERS AWAIT

Can you let go of your history and step into the mystery?
—BUDDHIST TEACHING

once   we've   re-entered   the terrain

from whence we came

do we keep on evolving

rooting   sprouting   branching?

or is   all sensory   and   spiritual work   done?

is   growing   complete?

is   our   solitary mission   accomplished?

TREMBLING

...till I am carried away
trembling with joy.
—Uvavnuk, Inuit Nation

countless   ways   abide

to close out   this   gracious grind

wish   trembling with joy

RETURNING TO GOD

And the dust returns to the earth as it was,
and the spirit returns to God who gave it.
—Ecclesiastes 12:7

love is the   governing energy   of my   universe

the divine power that grants life

graces and goads

yea   sustains us

and   will surely   surround us   upon   our   last   breath

call   it   what you will

God or Love or…?

only   the   reality   matters

A DEATHRIGHT

When it is time to help a loved one face death, may we not distract
them from a deathright, from the natural process of enlightenment,
of dying into grace. May we allow them to turn their attention to the
natural order of the universe, to the Center, to Spirit.
May we not do something but just be there.
—Kathleen Dowling Singh

the moment   arrives   when   we the living   need

to   stop   pleading

cease fixing

and   simply allow   our dying   companion

to   withdraw   naturally
say goodbye in   their   own way   own time
flow onward

transition

into   the realm of   the beyond

the   embrace   of   the   Oversoul

BE A GOOD ANCESTOR

Be a good ancestor, stand for something bigger than yourself,
and add value to the Earth during your sojourn.
—MARIAN WRIGHT EDELMAN

impossible   to conjure   generations ahead
        easier   to imagine
                little ones
                        known and unknown

                                currently
climbing trees
        squealing   with delight   and fright

                    we belong   to an ancestry
            that owes   every last baby
                    fuller   access   to
                        shelter   education
health   hope
        an   all-out   chance
                to

        touch the sky
                                their   very   own   sky

THE DOOR INTO THE DARK

Leave the door open for the unknown, the door into the dark.
That's where the most important things come from,
where you yourself came from,
and where you will go.
—Rebecca Solnit

we arise   from   the darkness

of   our   mother's   womb

full-force   into   blast   of   brightness

we spend   entire lifetimes   juggling

vagaries   of   a dark-light   universe

when   our time   to die   arrives

we   re-enter   the darkness

of   our   Mother Earth

POTLACH

winter crossroads
        invokes
    Native American ritual

      the   *giveaway*

        other   animals   do   it

buffaloes   bestow   all   their   parts
      flesh
        hide
          horns
            for   the   benefit   of   kindred

    trees   compost   the soil

creation   summons   all   two-leggeds
      to sow
        plant
          reap
   give   away   the   bounty   of   our   being

SMALL BUT GOOD

My world is small but good.
—MARY FLANAGAN TOWLE

mom   luminous   with   age

spent the last two weeks of her almost 96 years
        at a pre-selected convalescent home
                alongside   two other   farewell voyagers

in a room with   bedside table
        upon which stood   photographs   of husband   Harold
                sons   Phil and Tom
        bible   wide-open   to favorite passage
                                and

butcher paper sheet   taped to the wall   posting
granddaughter's claim

"Grandma, do you know how much you are loved!"

SUMMATION

I don't want to get to the end of my life and find that I have lived
just the length of it. I want to have lived the width of it, as well.
—Diane Ackerman

the bell tolls for thee

each self   straight-away   mounts scales

for   final   weigh-out

DEAD BUT NOT GONE

*Those who are dead are never gone: they are in the tree that rustles,
in the wood that groans, in the water that sleeps, in the breast of the
woman, in the child who is wailing, the grasses that weep,
in the whispering rocks, in the forest.*
—BIRAGO DIOP, SENEGALESE POET AND STORYTELLER

we   perish   physically

our bodies   scatter   to the winds   tumble   earthward

but   our souls   survive

in myriad   ways   sites

known   and   unknown

foreign

and   familiar

EXIT WORDS

if   given the opportunity

what might   *your*   exit words   be

to a nurse   the kind one   as well as   the surly one

someone   long dead   still purring

to   an   unreconciled friend   furious family member

to   an   animal   not your own

to   an unborn child   in   a   foreign land?

HOKA HEY

Today is a good day to die, "hoka hey" (all is accomplished).
—LAKOTA TRIBE

let go   let be   let

all   the climbing   is over

relinquish   body

HANDIWORK

To receive everything, one must open one's hands and give.
—Taisen Deshimaru

suffering is alleviated

one hand on   one hand out   one hand up

at a time

joy is amplified

one hand on   one hand out   one hand up

at a time

hands were created to console and celebrate

from birth   to death   and beyond

MORTAL

It is important that when we come to die,
we have nothing to do but to die.
—CHARLES HODE

kids   aren't   thinking   about   death
understandable

in fact   much of the time   teens think   they're   invincible
so i pass on   a few   well-worn tips   to   minors   near and far

one day
your skin   will sag and blotch
your mind   will drift
your tree   will decay
you   will croak

so   my sweet and guileless   juveniles

wrap up every day   as cleanly   constructively   as possible

dare to rub   some irritations   into pearls
before   you   perish

TRUE RELIGION

True religion is surrender.

—Mohammed

everything has been felt   thought   preached   done
experienced   in the name of religion
    ecstasy   brutality   compassion   subservience
              best   and   worst   of humanity

religion means
                at   its   truest   and   most profound
        shedding physicality
                releasing outcomes
                    canning biases
abandoning dreams   even posthumous hopes

    surrendering   our very all
        back   back   back
            to   an
                ever-expanding

            Cosmos

YOU

*What if, as death approached, you found there was, after all,
nothing to be frightened of? What if we began to feel contentedly
part of the great cycle of nature (please, take my carbon atoms)?*
—Julian Barnes

you are superb gift

remarkable   creation

one last job   feed earth

ENDURE...THAT'S ALL

*Cancer is to be endured, that's all. The best you can hope for is to fend
it off, like a savage dog, but cancer isn't defeated; it only retreats, is held
at bay, retires, bides its time, changes form, regroups.*

—Brian Doyle

it's not only cancer

there   exist   other   unavoidable disasters
unconquerable torments
                ruined relations
                    blown ambitions
                        unfixables

exercise   while cutting   Alzheimers in half   sometimes

                        won't prevent it
    prayer   only   consoles

    homo sapiens must
            make sufficient treaty
                    with what's achievable
                        what endures

UNFINISHED

I'm constantly re-evaluating, open to new ideas and ways.
I'm not the same person I was a day ago.
—Grace Boggs, at 96

wandering and wondering
down
winding pathway

laden with poignant
recollections
cruel
infirmities
seaworthy
hopes
rising
hush
toward
one looming certainty

we all breast the tape

unfinished

Growing All the Way to Our Grave

RAZE AND REBUILD

*The Ise Grand Shinto Shrine in Japan is completely razed
and rebuilt every 20 years.*

—(FIRST IN 690, LATEST IN 2013)

i don't likely have two decades left

but surely possess

20 months

days

hours

minutes

within which to overhaul

at least modify

my homestretch   penchants   and   predilections

SAVING PANDO

A tree is not a forest. On its own, it is at the mercy of wind and weather. But together, many trees create a protected ecosystem that enables them to live to be very old.

—Peter Wohlleben

we   are   trees
standing   solitary
as   well   as   flourishing   in   groves

like our kinsfolk
the Pando species in Utah
a single   quaking aspen with one massive   underground
root system

80,000 years old   and garlanded   with the heaviest
known organism
in   the   world

currently beset by   drought   insects   disease

we are laboring to save Pando
even as we labor to save the greater globe
even as we labor to save ourselves

often   from   ourselves

LEAVING

leaving behind wares

leaving behind family

leaving behind pals

leaving behind memories

leaving everything behind

WHILE STILL KICKING

East Asian death poems are

traditionally composed upon one's death bed

delivering last words   so to speak

noble   fitting   climax

but   pen-ultimate reflections   on mortality

count   too

plentiful   things

to feel   say   write   do

while   still   kicking

SOMETIMES

sorrows   just persist

hurts stab   inerasable

pains permeate core

nearing death   we seek relief

sometimes   we depart   throbbing

KEEP THE GIFT MOVING

Love doesn't die, people do;
so when all that's left of me is love,
give me away.
—Anonymous

love triumphs
     only
         if we keep the gift moving
            every where
        every time
         every how

   until   our   embodied love   expires
        is buried
           and   buds

      a   subsequent   blush
           of

       growth

THE THREE L'S

In the end these things matter most:
How well did you love?
How fully did you live?
How deeply did you let go?
—BUDDHA

other   pertinent   questions   hover

yet

pale

next   to the three L's

loving   well

living   fully

letting   go   deeply

LAST MOMENTS

When death finds you, make sure it finds you alive.
—African Proverb

what might our closing hour be like?

difficulty breathing
          afraid
             alert
                    craving to communicate
                         or retreat
        hopeful
            prickly
               tranquil

              who knows   who knows?

if given my druthers
        if my mind is sentient
          if my heart beats
            if my voice pulsates in the slightest
       i hope to warble
              a medley of melodies
        singing   my   way   back   home

"IT'S OVER"

baseball   hall-of-famer   and   malapropism wizard
      ("it's déjà vu all over again")

was asked   "What inscription would you like on your tombstone?"

           Yogi Berra ventured seven letters
               "It's over"

well   i   wonder
    when i spill   into my grave

   when my specific tree   falls   crumbles   disperses
         will   there be   more?

  although the self isn't permanent   are we annihilated?

does one live on in some alternate form or fashion?

          is it really over   Yogi?

CHOICE

Growing older does not necessarily mean becoming wiser or kinder.
Many die jealous, bitter, and angry. It's a choice.
—Gary Zukav

aging poses   so does dying

in copious guises

one critical choice

in the face   of   remorse   anxiety

bewilderment

to   soften

or harden

opinions   belly   being?

TAKING THE PLUNGE

Why not go down…into the lake, consciously, like Beowulf.
Don't die on the shore.
—David Whyte

for one who nearly drowned as a young boy

    thrown into   the deep end   by rambunctious lads

    i exhibit   unshakeable fright   around

    bodies of water

nonetheless

    at this juncture in life

taking an occasional plunge   into uncharted   spiritual rapids

    piques my curiosity

    preps me   for the eventual

    plummet

OWE NOTHING

Owe no one anything, except to love one another.
—ROMANS 13:8

plow through

        all your belongings   cupboards   files   accounts

              odds and ends

                care-fully

take your time   no rush

      you're   still   cogent   full of it   in charge

see whom you owe

      money

           a conciliatory word

                clothes   crystal   artifacts

an overdue embrace   a moldy meaningful volume

      deliver   them   personally

           reckon up

                  leave life

        debt-free

DUBBING DEATH

It's not that I'm afraid to die.
I just don't want to be there when it happens.
—WOODY ALLEN

what   might   one   dub   death?

last hooray

      going home

          final goodbye

              melting into God

                    rest assured

                        fare thee well

                            tasty to the last drop

                        off to a better world

              gone

          clear light

shuffling off the mortal coil

      into the everlasting arms

          another country

            de-animation

              heaven

                    from dust to dust

                      sayonara

A SELF IN EVOLUTION

I am and will be until I die, a self in evolution.
—George Sheehan

minstrels   when asked
        to read their   "best"   poem
                often resort   to something   tried and true

i side with the bard
            who mused:
                        "my best piece hasn't been written yet!"

restless aspirants
negotiating precipitous slopes
buffeted by swirling fancies
mounting   branch   by   branch   by   branch
        destination   always   couple   climbs   ahead

        meandering
                among   peaks   of
                    was
                            is
                                    shall be

BELOVED

The beloved shall grow old, go ill, and be taken away finally.
No matter how tenderly we love, how bitterly we argue,
how cunningly we hide, this is what shall happen.
—Mary Oliver

one of us   will go first   my beloved

if it is i   please convey   to any gathered grieving

a portion   of   what and who   i tried to resemble

and   if it is you

don't blush   or   shush   me

let the world   receive an earful   of   your feats

and   my   undying   fondness

LISTO

Spanish term which means: smart, clever, ready, and prepared.

too many folks are   waiting around to die
           rather than   getting ready to die

          the distinction matters

    instead of lounging about
       losing spark
          sputtering
               coasting

stay   vibrant and animated   true-to-your-life

      mustering intentional goodbyes
being emotionally current
         making amends
      "packing all your bags"   as   Pope John   urged

    summing   up   before   shuffling   off

WARM-UP

Die before you die.

—Mohammed

this sobering　　　useful　　　verity
　　　seconded　by　Socrates
　　　then　Montaigne　　　as well

　　　impels all mortals
　　　　to practice dying

releasing　　some　thing
　　　　　some　want
　　　　　　　some　one

　　　　　　　　　　daily

　　staying　　in sound　spiritual form
　　　　for

　　our　　subsequent　crossing

GRAVELY MISS

The way of death whispers in your ear:
"There is only love."
—KAREN WYATT

lounging on our daughter's living room couch
while she and my wife interior decorate

i pop up for periodic lifting
but basically bask
in their   high-spirited   fragrant   cheery   chatter

soaking   up   the unmistakable timbre   of   each   voice

i will   sooner or later

gravely
gravely   miss

SATISFIED?

If this were your last day, would you be satisfied?
—Lewis Mumford

since we don't know when our last day will come

there's an urgency   to the what   and   how of every day

with which   we're endowed

my unembellished aim   is   to be satisfied

make that   sufficiently satisfied

what's   yours?

let's swap notes

NAKED

And when the day arrives for the final voyage
and the ship that never returns is set to sail,
you'll find me aboard, traveling light,
with few possessions, almost naked,
like the children of the sea.
—Antonio Machado

some   enjoy   short stints   on earth

some   medium-length   spells

some   long-term   jaunts

    yet same kismet

      awaits

    we arrive bare

     we don clothes

      we depart naked

CIRCLING

the   grand   finale   is   strikingly
distinct from earlier dances

the childhood twirl
the youthful boogie
the adult jive
the mid-life waltz

swaying   whirling
with   cautious abandon

circling   the   drain

then   entering   the   drain

MILLIONTH OF AN INCH

Our job is to move the world a millionth of an inch.
—GARY SNYDER

we grow up   with mammoth dreams
     such as   moving mountains
       albeit   shovelful by shovelful

when we join   home-stretchers united   and start paying our dues

   aspirations grow   less grandiose
     our movements   measured   more
       in inches   than mounds   or   miles

              ensouling
   a   good enough   a   worthy enough   life
             when
   blanketed   with   loam

BREATH

You thought you were dust and now you find you are breath.

—Rumi

true treasure   breathing

blessing   from start to finish

breathing stops   then what?

TREE-LIKE

Buddha meditated under a tree, was enlightened under a tree,
and died lying down between two trees.
—Norman Fischer

words   can assist   in guiding   our destinies

truth   *trust*   *truce*   *tree*

are rooted   in the same old   Germanic and English
clump of terms

reminding   all creatures   to be tree-like
during our earthly escapade

solid   strapping   bendable   upright

whether planting trees
sitting under trees
walking like trees
or
re-fertilizing the ground

COMPANIONS

Take good care, as you walk one another home.

—Ram Dass

humaneness   requires

partnering   fellow creatures

morn   through   evening

but remember   walk don't run

compassionate   companions

GROUND

Ground is immediate and authentic, beneath our feet...
ultimate substance in which all things stand.
—CHRISTOPHER ALEXANDER

during our twilight years
life's primarily about
ground

finding

solid   ground
common   ground
battleground
safe ground
tilling ground
sacred ground

returning to the ground of our being

A BENEDICTION

The trees in a forest care for each other, sometimes even nourishing the stump of a felled tree for centuries after it was cut down by feeding it sugars and other nutrients, and so keeping it alive.
—TIM FLANNERY

may the sun and the moon

a grove of trees   perhaps   one woolly animal

plus   frank   faithful
amigos
surround   me   when   i am   dying

then

may   my   fallen log

leave   an ingrained mark   on nature's canvass
perchance   host   a smidgen   of   greenery

UNCLENCHING OUR FISTS

The night kissed the fading day with a whisper.
"I am death, your mother, from me you will get new birth."
—Rabindranath Tagore

the rabbis of olden days posited
we come into this world with our fists clenched

and when the time of exodus arrives
our hands are flung free

during the interval
as we grow up and on
our earthly vocation   is   to open   wide   our hands

accepting the outlier
massaging the maimed
managing strenuous experiences
fostering tangible intimacy

handing   up   on   forth

unclenching   our   fists

MOTHERLY CARESS

Death, hold out your arms for me.
Embrace me,
give me your motherly caress.
—Helen Dunmore

most of us
    rarely succumb
        of   a   broken   heart

    but   plenty   enter tombs
       full
           of   cumulative   rubble

       pining   for   motherly caress

NEXT TIME

next time you greet   any   and all   vegetation

take a moment   several moments   all the time you need

to   shower thanks

upon forests   that make

our   atmosphere   more   breathable

they are under   dire threat

so are we

SHOJI

Life and death are a package deal. You can't really pull them apart.
In Japanese Zen, the term "shoji" translates as life-death.
We cannot be truly alive without maintaining an awareness of death.
—FRANK OSTASESKI

notice   oh notice   fellow traveler
     deeply
        dearly
   everything
     within   and   beyond   your temple

bathe   in life's   briny sea   of   irrepeatables

   soon   soon enough   your single jaunt
       on earth
          above earth

      will   be   replete

WEEP

Confucius wept.
Confucius when he understood
that he would soon die,
wept.

i   too   will likely   weep

upon   the appearance   of the grim reaper

fountains   of   tears

tears of   mourning   joy   sympathy   wrath   tenderness

appreciation

ANXIETY ATTACK

having spent lots of time in nursing homes

first   as minister   now as singer

i sporadically

suffer a   minor   anxiety attack

Gertrude isn't here today

Pedro died last week

where is Willie

maybe mortality is catching in this room?

until i   remember

i already have what these dear ones have

we're all   as the poet says   terminal on this ward

DEAD SILENT

parents   don't wish   to burden   or worry   offspring

children   aren't ready   to talk   about it

friends back away

the   room   stands

dead silent

until   the shadows   fall

SAY THANK YOU

Say thank you rather than please when facing death.
—Annie Dillard

there's a time and place to beg and barter
      during the tattered course   of our travels
it's part of our human make-up
      to   want and wish   hope and fancy
          crave   and   covet something
    more stability   more knowledge

but not   when we're completing   our earthly circuit

dying   is the time   to burst forth
      in sheer gratitude

for a life   utterly   unexpected   unearned

MEMENTO MORI
REMEMBER, YOU HAVE TO DIE.

welcome   to   the   grand equalizer

just when   you're prone   to deny   or tame   it
just when   you think   you can   outwit   or   beat   it
death   comes up   and   bites you   in the butt

generals and slaves
presidents and plebeians
are bitten

a sobering comfort
to realize   that   no matter wealth   status
trophies   or   burdens

our   eventual   fortunes
are   equivalent

A FRUITFUL EXERCISE

it's   a fruitful exercise   to compose our
                own tributes   this side of the grave

commence   with a   six-word memoir
        summing up   one's life
            e.g.   "struggled mightily to major in kindness"

        then   shape   a   page-long   obituary notice

when ready   take a long nap   a longer stroll
        then   rough out notes
            for eulogizers   to work with
                    once   you're   dead

they   may   not   heed   your   lead
after all   you're no longer around   to make amendments

        but   at least   they'll know   roughly
                who   you thought   you   were

THEN THERE WILL BE LOVE

If one knows that what is born will end in death,

then there will be love.

—Sutra of Buddha

when we confess that being born

begins the inevitable road toward death

it can make   one   a   gentler

pleasanter   itinerant

every monarch   every guru

every scoundrel   every saint

has been   an   infant   propelled toward   its very demise

YES

Death is our friend precisely because it brings us into absolute and
passionate presence with all that is here, that is natural,
that is love...Life always says Yes and No simultaneously.
Death (I implore you to believe) is the true Yea-sayer.
It stands before eternity and says only: Yes.
—Rainer Maria Rilke

when we   die too young   or terribly

death   is   no   friend

however

now   at the cusp   of a   lengthy excursion

i'm grooming   my heart and soul

to

voice   the   Yes

ALL IS GRACE

Karl Rahner's finishing words on this earth,
uttered with startling authority and joy
for someone minutes from death, were: "All is grace!"
—BRIAN DOYLE

when all is said and done
after slogging   through   swamps of   dread   and   ecstasy
periods   of being   ungraceful   and   ungracious

we humanoids   are   still   fortunate
statistical miracles
privileged   to have been around   at all

to have experienced   any seasons
of   splendor   and   emptiness

all is grace

LIGHT

as rapidly   as our individual light   goes out

it is subsumed   in the   continuing light

of a   fathomless   universe

wondrous phenomenon

our light   glistens   forth

in the sun   descendants   the stars

our   sparkle   no longer named

shines   on

FUTURE NOT OUR OWN

We are workers not master builders, ministers not messiahs.
We are prophets of a future not our own.
—ARCHBISHOP OSCAR ARNULFO ROMERO
(MURDERED, MARCH 24, 1980)

think now   of your fading life   as a legacy   an endowment   a gift
ponder less   what   you've achieved
and more
the foundations   you've   laid
the   footprints   you've   forged

suckling   unknown   tomorrows

life does not end with our end

we are waves   in an   ongoing ocean

branches   on   the   Tree of Life

TRANSITION

Life is pleasant. Death is peaceful. It's the transition that troubles me.
—Isaac Asimov

dying   will snatch us away   in its own time
                its   own   inscrutable fashion

maybe painful
        maybe   soothing

but   death is not mean
                or an outlier
                    or a failure
neither an enemy to be conquered nor   a prison to be escaped

death just is   as life just is

a series of transitions   one after another
colossal   tiny   awkward   desirable ones

culminating   in   the   transition of
                transitions

LIVING-AND-DEAD YOKED

We live on dead people's heads.
Scratching under a suburb of St. Louis,
archaeologists recently found thirteen settlements,
one on top of the other,
some of which lasted longer
than St. Louis.
—ANNIE DILLARD

weirdly related

archaeologically hinged

heads   on top   of heads

SHARED DESTINY

travel   meticulously

                    admiringly

                              from   a place   of   thankfulness

        encountering   moreover engaging

                              perchance

for the last time

                every stone   sprig   soul

                          animate   inanimate   reality

                    in   full recognition

        that   you are brothers   and   sisters   in   death

        that   you   cradle   the   same   fate

CONSCIOUSLY

Only that day dawns to which we are awake.
—Henry David Thoreau

to die as consciously as possible
awakened and authentic
responsive   and   accountable

no guarantee   only a hope

yet

if we can't   go out   consciously

we   can   carry on   consciously

this   very instant

FINAL SALUTE

what will be your   final salute   to a dying companion?

paying respects   at the funeral   is crucial   but   too late
    viewing the coffin   may occur   but s/he isn't really there
they   won't hear   firecrackers   or   any   21-gun-salute

            so

    be ready and willing   to show up   as your buddy   is dying
                participate in a bedside vigil
        (if   that   is   what
                the dying person   wishes)

            words

                tears

                    touch

                        silence

        mainly attend   bear witness

FALLEN

nearby   our home   in uptown San Diego

dwells a   verdant canyon   laden with   lush foliage

wild rodents   a   migratory stream

piles   of fallen trees

strewn   across

luxuriant   landscape

today   i view them   with deeper reverence

even hug   a couple   fallen warriors

for   someday   i will lie down   beside them

ETERNAL BLISS?

i find most notions of eternal life or paradise singularly uninteresting
it would be nice   in many cases   (although not all)
to reconnect with   departed friends   or loved ones
but not to stomach   an interminable sameness
of our bonds

without the presence   of exertion   even   sorrow
perpetual existence   would prove
oppressively bland

did you ever hear an evangelist describe heaven in terms of the
challenges   waiting to be faced   or in terms
of passion   or toil   or justice?
no   it's always   an Elysian Fields

characterized   by   terrible constancy
with no further   growth or change   taking place
destitute of variation or wrestling

how boring   eternally boring

TEACH US TO NUMBER...

Teach us to number our days that we might
apply our hearts unto wisdom.
—Psalm 90:12

the Psalmist   reminds us   that we're   all   like grass

that the years   of our lives   may be   three score and ten

or   maybe   with providence   four score   or   more

pay heed   to   your daily   blessings-and-curses

number   your seasons   on earth

infinite   they're   not

counting them   spurs   us to   render   wiser   choices

reckoning   is   an encouragement   to live

with   gratefulness   mettle   appetite

I PRAISE A WORLD

i   praise   a   world   that   will   not   be   forever

if   we   were   to   be here   forever
        there'd be   no reason   to take   special notice
of   this   virginal   Spring
        there'd be   an   infinity   of Springs   to notice
so it wouldn't matter   if we missed one   or two   or   a dozen

    if we're going to live forever
it doesn't matter   if we miss   a person   or two
        there will always   be time   for other people

    on the contrary   it's because   we don't   have an eternity
with one another   that we must   seize the time   for one another

how many of us would clean up the environment
        grow a beloved community
            nurture healthy children
    do anything   of much importance
        if we believed   we had an eternity   in which to do it?

A GOOD DEATH

Grudges get heavier the longer they're carried.
—P. K. Thomajan

a good death   permits us   to be   pretty much
the same person dying
              as   we were   when we're alive

a good death   doesn't mean i'll die peacefully   although i'd like that

a good death   is more than   going to sleep one night
and not waking up
              although   i'll   take   that   too

a good death   is extinction   with significance

a good death   doesn't contradict   the conduct of   my vocation
                       partnership
                              family
                                  way of life

a good death   is   when i go   into the ground
essentially clean
       of   regrets   and   resentments
                ruddy   with   rejoicing

DEATH'S JUSTICE

Death is a camel that lies down at every door.
Sooner or later you must ride the camel.
—ARAB PROVERB

death's justice   greets   all

no good deed   excuses   you

strikes   indiscriminately

makes room   for   other creatures

to   arrive   nourish the soil

SEE WHAT REMAINS

Let come what comes, let go what goes. See what remains.
—Ramana Maharshi

as exit approaches

don't plead

don't predict

don't panic

welcome

what comes

what goes

what remains

SCARS

God will not look you over for medals,
degrees, or diplomas, but for scars.
—Elbert Hubbard

discolored   bruises

nasty   scabs   bashes   welts   bumps

badges   of   honor

SPILLING OUT OUR TREASURE

I would like to believe when I die that I have given myself away
like a tree that sows seeds every spring and never counts the loss,
because it is not loss, it is adding to future life…
strongly rooted, perhaps, but spilling out its treasure on the wind.
—MAY SARTON

i would relish   my death to   "add to future life"
    that's my   plan   wish   legacy

but   why wait

can't   i   "spill out my treasure on the wind"
     this side of the grave

sow   a few oats
     seeds
       here   and   now?

FULL VESSEL

On the day when death will knock at thy door,
what wilt thou offer death?
I will set before my guest the full vessel of my life.
I will never let death go with empty hands.
—RABINDRANATH TAGORE

what constitutes   "the full vessel of my life"?
what do i wish to share with my final guest?

i'm pondering   pondering

well   most assuredly

a heart full of thanksgiving
a   confession or two
ample waterworks

my full vessel
streaming   freely

ETHICAL WILL

Patriarch Isaac, recognizing his days are
numbered, calls his first born to him.
He charges Esau, "so that I may give you my blessings before I die."
—GENESIS 27

near   our   worldly   wind-up
there comes the opportunity
to   call   our clan   together
(you   name   the   qualifiers)

all at once   or one by one by one by one
to unveil an ethical will

conveying to   dear ones   nimbly   serenely
the   values and visions
you esteem

then turning   folks loose
to   live the lives
they   must   personify

on their own

Growing All the Way to Our Grave

EULOGY

Don't aim for grandiosity; instead pursue the small and telling stroke,
the bull's eye detail.
—Ron Marasco

when honoring the deceased

we gravitate toward hyperbole

so that mourners barely recognize the body in the casket

a gushing   syrupy   idealized portrait   does no one justice

pay   honest and proper   homage

to each idiosyncratic

never-before   never-again   mortal

EQUALLY HOLY FORCES

There is no cure for birth and death save to enjoy the interval.
—George Santayana

every love bond   from birth   forward   ends in
          departure
              divorce
                    death

              mindfulness
                    entails   growing accustomed
                                        to leaving and being left

          salute   birth and death   as equally holy forces

                  go forth   and hail   eternity   now

THE TREES KNOW IT

Someone has died, even the trees know it.
—ANNE SEXTON

human losses   mount

     jarring   our very   bases

the dogs   smell   death

     insects   are   on alert

    the   breeze   grasps   every   fatality

even the trees know it

when they are lugged   and   logged   away   into lumber

may we   return the sentiment

LEFT ME FOR DEAD

My life is poured out like water, and all my bones are out of joint.
My heart is like wax, melting within me. My strength has dried up
like sunbaked clay. My tongue sticks to the roof of my mouth.
You have laid me in the dust and left me for dead.

—PSALM 22: 14-15

sometimes   our lives   are completely   whacked

our   moods are   sour   cranky-to-ornery
our   body   is   beyond repair
our   soul   is   stricken
lamentations   shriek   skyward

nothing to live for

we are done   we are left for dead

one request dominates

"O God   let me go   quickly!"

WHEN WE DIE

She whom we love and lose is no longer where she was before.
She is now wherever we are.
—St. John Chrysostom (349-407)

when we die
what about those left behind
the survivors

does our life   merely   drive them
to
perpetual mourning
periodic visits to   photo albums   graveyards
or does it   grant them   invigoration   purposefulness?

the dead   need not   be glorified
only dignified

by the quality of
the lives of   survivors
moving forward

humming   a   fragment   of   their   melody

HOPING FOR A PEEP HOLE

When your world dies around you, you know it's time to go.
You just get tired, but I hope there is a peep hole
up there in heaven to be able to spy
on my family and friends!

how can one argue   with my friend's mother's
dying wish   it's a way of extending your peculiar life-drama right?

but   of course   lots of "what if-s"   linger
what if   your personal consciousness dies   when you die
what if   your destination is down below   rather   than up above
what if spying is deemed illegal or off-limits   in either realm
what if   family or friends   don't want   you or anyone else
(dead or alive!) spying   on them?

and   clearly   there will   likely
be   an   in-law or out-law   who wishes
you   would   simply   shut   the peep up

Growing All the Way to Our Grave

DIE IN HARNESS

When my time comes, I hope I can die in harness,
still engaged in creative work.
—OLIVER SACKS

everyone's hope

yet   some will die   productive

others will   wash out

ON A RAINY SUNDAY

There are people who pray for eternal life
and don't know what to do with themselves
on a rainy Sunday.
—G. K. CHESTERTON

cease focusing   upon what   you didn't do
three decades ago

    halt predicting   what   life-after-death   will
    or won't   provide

        take care of   business   including any monkey-business

            this   sunny   Thursday

                    this   rainy   Sunday

INTO THE UNKNOWN

A Zen student queried her master as to what happens after death.
The master smiled and said, "I do not know." "How can that be?
You are a Zen master." "Yes, but I am not a dead Zen master!"

agnosticism

we   know   not   what   happens   next

die   then   be surprised

DEEP PEACE

Deep peace to your bones...
it is final now
sleep your untroubled and true dream.
—Antonio Machado

may death be like this

      carcass   resting untroubled

alongside   a true   dream

CHI

chi   is the vital force   in the universe
breath of life
pervading   all facets   of existence

when we die
part of us   (the body)   returns   to the earth
while   (our spirit) lives   on in the heavens   as *chi*
becoming   one   with the cosmos

ancestors   and   descendants   woven together
boundaries   fluid
death   not an ending   but a stage in the continuum of infinitude

we
remain   integral parts   of   the universal energy

so   some   say

SINGING IN NURSING HOMES

Music and sound weave a magic carpet for the soul's journey home.
—Don Campbell

when residents   approach   death

words can help

presence   is   an inordinate gift

yet   singing   like nothing else

insinuates   itself into   the   full   corpus

i'm   currently   privileged

to be both   a life-room

and a   death-bed

crooner

GROW...GROW

Every blade of grass has its own angel bending over it,
whispering, "Grow, grow."
—Talmud

the root of   lost   is the Old English *losian*   meaning to perish
in today's parlance   being lost   merely means   not knowing
where we are

seniors   surely reside
in a state of   *losian*

nestled   somewhere   between   disorientation
and death

often anxious   wandering   out of place

wake up   comrade
make new   discoveries   brave   an unparalleled
direction

shape your   god-given   intentions
this side of death

grow   grow

grow all the way to your grave

PAIN

As my wife lies dying, I fully realize that love doesn't eliminate,
but simply neutralizes, the pain.
—Irv Polster

pain is obstinate

whether   living   or   dying

just   manageable

JUST THIS

Do you want to know what's in my heart?
From the beginning of time: just this! just this!
—RYOKAN TAIGU (1758-1831)

we humans crave stuff to be set in stone

our achievements   immortalized

our homes   chockfull   of   trophies

our   posterity secure

yet   life-and-death   brews   other plans

everything   and   everyone   is   impermanent

transient   passing   ephemeral

so   embrace   Zen in a nutshell

just this   just this   just this   just this

right now   right now   right now

STRAIGHT AHEAD

there's   the Zen story   of two   lost monks
wandering   and   wondering
along life's   circuitous pathway

happening   upon a crone
an   archetypal woman of   seeming sagacity

the two ask the one

where is   the way   the way   the way?

and the crone   confidently   replies

"straight ahead"

whether   rejoicing   struggling   roaming
aging   or   dying

travel   "straight ahead"

NIRVANA

When the heart is without anxiety or obstruction then there is no fear.
When confusion and illusion are distant, that is true Nirvana.
—HEART SUTRA

in Hindu tradition
Nirvana signals the state of   perfect quietude and
freedom from *samsara*

the repeated rounds of rebirth

i doubt   if many   of us   will ever   reach
this liberated   condition
at least   i'm   not banking   on it

but that   won't   keep   this temporal pilgrim   from achieving
a   heightened sense   of inner serenity   and   outer
compassion

before   valediction

CALL TO COURAGE

The only courage demanded of us is to have courage
for the most strange,
the most singular,
and the most inexplicable
that we may encounter.
—Rainer Maria Rilke

abundant   are   the astounding   challenges   we face   in living

but   none   is likely   to prove
as   curious
historic

or inexplicable

as dying

so   elders   crones
start mustering
all   your courage

far in advance

YOU MATTER

You matter because you are you,
and you matter to the end of your life.
—Dame Cecily Saunders
Founder of the Hospice Movement, 1960

unique   gift   at birth

   full-bore   god-send   during   life

      you   matter   at   death

FINAL HUMAN ACT

Living while dying is our final human act....a divine art.
—Karen Speerstra

how   might   we die   with   a   measure   of   purpose

what can   we artfully   say   do   be

during   our   concluding   performance

on   life's   stage?

PRIZES

All anybody needs to know about prizes is that Mozart never won one.
—Henry Mitchell

yes   my beloved and i have   created   a   memorabilia room

filled   to the brim

with   photos   articles   honors   certificates   journals

yet   questions   nag   away

will anyone choose to poke through this stuff?

how much of our real worth is contained in that room?

how long will our keepsakes stay intact?

any award ceremonies in the afterlife?

ON THE SHELF

I leave my place to the young, the talented, and the ambitious.
And I willingly accept life on the shelf.
—WILLIAM STAFFORD

i'm not willing to accept life on the shelf
just yet   or   maybe   ever

being shelved sounds   too much like being   tossed aside
warehoused

after my departure
my hope differs

may the core   of my being   reside   less on any   shelf

more inside   a few hearts

for   awhile

OPEN DOOR POLICY

If a gate stands open long enough, it can't be closed again.
—Ted Kooser

there are doors   that need to be flung shut   prior to
final adieu
    doors   on   vanished dreams   drawn-out resentments

nonetheless
      certain fragile   flawed   love bonds   persist
          where willing or not   mutual or not

i choose   to pursue   some-sort-of   resolution

        i refuse   to close   every door

in due course
          let death   do   that

BIRTH AND DEATH

The Real People nation has for centuries had the practice of speaking at birth and at death the same phrase to one and all:
"We love you and support you on the journey."
—MARLO MORGAN

launch   lives   lovingly

swathe   with love   throughout the course

love once more   at close

SPEND THE AFTERNOON

Spend the afternoon. You can't take it with you.
—Annie Dillard

you may recall the Jewish admonition to repent
one day before you die
"but i won't know when that is"
retorts the cynic

well   my friends   that's the point   isn't it?

we're   prodded   to repent as well as exult
to enhance rather than diminish
our life   all life
every   day   today

because   we   can't   be   sure
that   it   won't   be   our   last   lap

THOROUGHLY USED UP

I want to be thoroughly used up when I die...
—George Bernard Shaw

no   time   to   hold back

    resist   refresh   yea   rejoice

      leave   your all   on field

HEARD

If a tree falls in the forest,
and there is no one
to hear it, is there a sound?
—Jehookah Jarmon, Ukraine

when   any tree falls earthward
there   is   hearable noise
the   crash of   timber
the   gasp of   sorrow

when   any   human being   falls   earthward
grave marker   or not
there is   the detectable   loss
of life

every creation
precious
heard

FOUR CARDINAL VIRTUES

There are four cardinal virtues: humility, humility, humility, humility.
—St. Bernard

we materialize   from   the humus

realize   our full   humanity
                     through   sparkling   humor
                              steady   humaneness
                              bedrock   humility

                    in   due   course
                                        re-entering
                                            the

                    humus

TOMBSTONE TEST

Each person's life can be summed up in one sentence,
and it should be one that has an active verb.
—CLARE BOOTH LUCE

perhaps you've heard of the tombstone test

wherein

you write your name

date of birth

scribble   a substantial dash

predict   the imagined year   (maybe even the day)

of   your   death

then   hew   a sentence that you'd like   scrawled   on your
gravestone

a spot-on   clear-cut   dynamic   line

BAD STUFF

Whatever bad stuff has happened to you in this life, you have to do three things: accept it; be kind to it; and let it be kind to you.
—Kerry Egan

harsh   wounds   stab us all

none   exits   life   unscathed

seek   balm   of   kindness

DYING SOON

If you were going to die soon and had only one phone call
you could make, who would you call and what would you say?
And why are you waiting?

—STEPHEN LEVINE

as   our time   runs   on   out

duty   arrives

to   place   our   spiritual house   in order

make   that   critical   connection

submit   something   soulful

dawdle   not

EAT CHOCOLATE NOW

Eat chocolate now. After you're dead, there isn't any.
—Jean Powell

go fly a kite

burst into laughter

compose a missive

cuddle an animal

devour   your   favorite sweets

life-after-death   life-after-life

wholly   uncertain

IT'S VERY DIFFICULT

I'm trying to die correctly, but it's very difficult, you know.
—Lawrence Durrell

dying properly

acceptably

may   not   lie   in   our   cards

so

settle for dying

with   adequate   grace

parcels   of   peace

wide-open   to   amazement

heartfully

TANHA

It is usually proclaimed that birth, aging, and death are suffering.
If we don't grasp (tanha), they are not suffering;
they are only bodily changes.
—AJAAN BUDDHADASA

tanha signals   an intense   futile thirst

an   irrational   physical and mental   pining

for   a   permanence   that   breeds suffering

we crave   longevity
rather   than relishing   each twinkle

we crave   utter security
which   only   spells imprisonment

we crave   this object   that   opportunity

cease   clinging   in   a world   of   change

be born   age   then die
breath-by-breath-by-breath-by-breath

LOVE THE END

To overcome deathophobia, we must learn to love the end.
—Stephen Jenkinson

my prayerful wish

would be

not merely to endure

but bear

even embrace

yea   love

my   one and only   earthly end

SUGATO

Buddhist term   meaning   "excellent realization"

path leading to freedom from suffering
off   to   a good   destination

referencing   an   idyllic   harmonious   result

during   life

or

a peaceful   sublime   departure   upon death

going-well

well-going

going-well

well-going

LET ME BE A DONKEY...

when   the Zen guide   was asked   what   his future life

would   be   like

he   candidly   claimed:

"let me   be a donkey   or a horse
and work   for   the   villagers!"

i resonate   with   the master

if my existence   extends   in   any   earthly form

i want   to be   employed   usefully

as a   practical   servant

an animal   that labors

LIKE A SAMURAI WARRIOR

To die "isagi-yoku" is one of the aspirations of the Japanese heart.
It means dying bravely, with a clear conscience, leaving no regrets...
—Daisetz T. Suzuki

during   whatever spiritual tussles   might accompany
my sendoff

my   major challenge   will be

to tread   the pathway   of   the   samurai warrior

facing death unflinchingly

ON THE SAME BRANCH

This late August day—
together on the same branch
dead leaves and live ones.

—Gary Thorp

living-and-dying

mingled   every   season

trees   humans   alike

THAT IS DEATH

Do you want to know how to die? Think of the thing
you treasure the most and drop it. That is death.
—Jiddu Krishnamurti

ponder the thing   or things

        bond   or bonds

                                most treasurable

                in   your   life-trunk

and let it   them   fade   melt away

        before   your   very eyes

                                drop

        beyond   your   very grasp

AFTERNOON TEA

Death is not the problem. Fear is. And fear is something we create.
—Julia Assante

as we   entertain   the prospect of   our own dying

what constitute   the most fearful demons

and are we willing   to invite   greet
converse with them

inside our hearts

for an imagined afternoon of tea

as the   cheeky   Tibetan yogi   Milarepa (1051-1135 CE)   did?

DANCE PARTNERS

on   woodblock prints   from the Middle Ages

death   is portrayed   as a skeleton

not as a   demon   or   foe

but   as bones   in motion

capering

frolicking

not with a   ghoul   or   phantom

but   with   a live   human being

death is our   dance partner

our   consort   at the cabaret

CREMAINS

Cremation is the combustion, vaporization, and oxidation of
cadavers to basic chemical compounds such as gases, ashes,
and mineral fragments retaining the appearance of dry bone.
—WIKIPEDIA

numerous are the   possible dispositions   of the body when we die
our exclusive job   is to   make   our own determination
in   consult with loved ones   beforehand

i   personally   prefer   cremation
but   have not chosen   precise   location   just yet

after   the   gracious   generous   grinding

my ashes   might be placed   in an old   cardboard   shoe box
formerly   cradling   prized baseball   cards

or in   an exquisite   festooned   urn
or   poured in the ground next to my beloved's
or scattered to the four winds

in a favorite forest   canyon   waterway

how about you   my friend?

LAMENT

For of all sad words of tongue or pen,
the saddest are these: "It might have been."
—John Greenleaf Whittier

research documents   that   greatest regret   of   those dying

is   having   lived   a   life

others

laid out   or   required   of   you

hence

mired   in   a   spiritual   sand trap

rather   than   fully embodying

your own   distinctive   reality

being   an   original

BUDDHA'S BLESSING

Be a light unto yourself, hold fast to the Truth.
Look not for refuge to anyone beside yourselves.
—BUDDHA'S LAST WORDS

we can   garner tips   even   considerable savvy   from others

and would be wise to do so

but   you and i   are   ultimately   our   own governors

the   prime authors   of our   storied existence

adopt   Buddha's   farewell advice   not   as   a burden

but   as   a   boost

yea   a blessing

CONTINUING MANIFESTATIONS

*When we lose someone we love, we should remember that the
person has not become nothing. Something cannot become nothing,
and nothing cannot become something. They have taken on another
form. That form may be a cloud, a child, or the breeze. We can see our
loved one in everything…in continuing manifestations. The body is
only the temporary home for our essence.*

—THICH NHAT HANH

when   i permit   myself   to turn   mystical

i   begin   to   experience   the presence

of   the deceased

in my   daily   sentiments   sensations

dead   need   not   mean   gone

reality can sustain in

evolving   forms   fresh   energy   unusual gifts

ceaseless transformations
"continuing manifestations"

DEATH DOULA

Doula comes from the modern Greek meaning "servant-woman."

formerly   *doulas*   were   birth companions
post-delivery   supporters

in   more   recent times   *doulas*   have become

end-of-life   soul midwives
transitional   coaches

lending hands   hearts   as folks leave   this earthly plane

bringing   succor   meaning
to
our closing daze

death doulas   (be they female or male)
help   usher   us   home

might you   be ready   willing   to request   a doula
or   become one   yourself?

CROSSING THE THRESHOLD

dying   skyward

dying   earthward

entering the light

entering the darkness

either route suits me fine

my   only   aspiration

is

returning

to

the

loving

source

of

all

LAST CHANCE

You only get one death. Live it.

—Bianca Nogrady

what might reside   on   your menu   of lasts?

last slice of pizza

last excursion to the forest

last concert

last walk with a dog

last full-body massage

last goodbye to dearest?

dying   would   present   last chance

to live   boldly   deliberately

admirably

TAKE WHATEVER COMES

When the tenth-century Chinese Zen master Dasui Fazhen was asked,
"How are you at the time when life-death arrives?"
he answered promptly, "When served tea, I take tea,
when served a meal, I take a meal."

a   graceful   exit

receive   whatever   presents

take   a meal   take   death

DEAD DEARS

Eugene was a most intimate friend of magic and a most captivating
friend of magicians. Because we need him still to be with us,
he is one of our treasured dead dears.
—ROBERT E. NEALE

there exist   the   dead

friends   family   foes

who   after   suitable homage   is paid

simply   slip   slip   slip   away

from   our   active   consciousness

then   there are   those   intimates

whom   we cannot shake   or   release

from our core

carried within   as long   as we   carry on

treasured   dead   dears

GO GENTLY

Do not go gentle into that good night,
old age should burn and rave at close of day;
rage, rage against the dying of the light.
—DYLAN THOMAS

surely   seniors   there is a time and place   to rant   and rave

as our doors   and   windows   squeak   slam shut

but if my   supreme desire   be told

i prefer to close out my existence

quietly   tenderly   peacefully

traveling   ever-so

gently

into   the   next realm

PLANT A TREE

Martin Luther (1483-1546)   German theologian   pivotal figure
in the Protestant Reformation

was asked   what   he would do   if   he knew   the world

was coming to an end

"i   would   plant   a   tree!"

good idea   righteous   deed

to seed   plant   harvest   any living entity
such as a tree

that hopefully   germinates

after the world

(at least   your world)

terminates

DONE IS DONE
—*Zen Buddhist Phrase*

when   a task   is completed

     when   a covenant   is struck

        when   a relationship   is irreparable

          when   the day   is over

            when   the coffin lid   closes

done   is   done

DEATH IS ON ITS WAY

*The Hopis give their young a "death chant" as they pass into
adolescence. It's a phrase they're taught to repeat every day, especially
at moments of danger and uncertainty. It is intended to assist them in
merging with the Great Spirit when they do die.*

—JOHN E. WELSHONS

in   our American culture   how are we preparing   our teenagers

for their   final fortune

are we   walking graveyards   talking last things

are   we gracing them   with death chants?

we prepare them for school
we prepare them for financial and social interactions
we prepare them for driving vehicles
we prepare them for dangers
we prepare them for sex and their vocations
we prepare them for life…altogether

how do we prepare them for dying

ours   theirs?

TEAM SPORT

Dying is a team sport.
—Timothy Leary

the dying process   defies predictability

often   confusing   messy   laden with quirks

this much   we know   to be true

dying   at its finest
is communal

the   head and heart   hands and heels

of   innumerable folks   are desired

professionals   family   strangers   buddies

are summoned
to carry   us   on home

SURRENDER

Dying is surrender to the earth and God's embrace.
—Teilhard de Chardin

helpless at birth   helpless at death

from   womb to tomb   vulnerable

precarious   beings

final assignment

surrender   to ground

to god

mysteries   that   fashioned   us

I OWE GOD A DEATH

*I've been lucky. I came from nowhere and had no reason to expect as
much from this one life as I've got. I owe God a death, and
the earth a pound or so of chemicals. Now let's see if
I can remember that when my time comes.*

—Wallace Stegner

we owe   God—this indescribably   marvelous universe
ourselves   and all creaturely companions   one death
especially   following   a   full and generous ride   into
elderhood

may this debt   be willingly   and   gladly   paid
when our turn comes   to join   the ground of all being

i say gladly   because we're   placed on earth   to find and
deliver joy

and   when our light finally goes out

if   we're   holy of heart

our souls   will echo   the glorious and calming scripture
from Isaiah 55:12

*for you shall go out in joy and be led forth in peace,
the mountains and the hills before you shall break forth into singing,
and all the trees of the field shall clap their hands.*

About Tom Owen-Towle

The Rev. Dr. Tom Owen-Towle has been a parish minister since 1967 and is the author of two dozen books on personal relationships and spiritual growth. Tom and his life-partner, the Rev. Dr. Carolyn Sheets Owen-Towle, are the active parents of four children and seven grandchildren. Tom is a guitarist, parlor magician, and currently sings with seniors, mentors children and youth, and volunteers with San Diego's homeless. Owen-Towle is a national leader who continues to conduct workshops and retreats on the core themes of his books.

FLAMING CHALICE PRESS publishes books on Unitarian Universalism, personal relationships, and spiritual growth. You can order copies of *Growing All the Way to Our Grave* on www.amazon.com. If you would like to contact Tom Owen-Towle, you may reach him through one of the following ways:

> Tom Owen-Towle
> 3303 Second Avenue
> San Diego, CA 92103
> Tel: (619) 933-1121
> Email: uutom@cox.net
> Web: www.tomo-t.com

Made in United States
Troutdale, OR
10/18/2023

13821544R00224